Living the Dream

Living the Dream

Joseph for Today

A Dramatic Exposition of Genesis 37 – 50

Pete Wilcox

LONDON ● COLORADO SPRINGS ● HYDERABAD

13 12 11 10 09 08 07   7 6 5 4 3 2 1

First published in 2007 by Paternoster
Paternoster is an imprint of Authentic Media
9 Holdom Avenue, Bletchley, Milton Keynes, Bucks, MK1 1QR
1820 Jet Stream Drive , Colorado Springs, CO 80921, USA
OM Authentic Media, Medchal Road, Jeedimetla Village,
Secunderabad 500 055, A.P., India
www.authenticmedia.co.uk
Authentic Media is a division of IBS-STL U.K., limited by guarantee, with its
Registered Office at Kingstown Broadway, Carlisle, Cumbria CA3 0HA.
Registered in England & Wales No. 1216232. Registered charity 270162

British Library Cataloguing in Publication Data

A catalogue record for this book is available from
the British Library.

ISBN-13: 978-1-84227-555-9

Design by James Kessell for Scratch the Sky Ltd. (www.scratchthesky.com)
Print Management by Adare Carwin
Printed in Great Britain by J.H. Haynes and Co., Sparkford

Contents

Introduction

The Joseph Story: A Text for Today

For centuries Jewish, Christian and Moslem parents, and more recently secular ones too, have called their children Joseph or Josephine: from Josephine Butler (the English social reformer) to Josef Stalin (the Russian dictator); from José Mourinho (the Portuguese football manager) to Giuseppe Garibaldi (the Italian revolutionary); from "Smokin' Joe" Frazier (the black American boxer) to Joseph Rowntree (the English industrialist and philanthropist). Some, like Yusuf Islam (formerly the musician Cat Stevens), have chosen the name for themselves. For the last five years (and probably longer than that) in both the UK and the USA, the name Joseph has featured among the 'Top Ten' most popular boys' names. Often the name has presumably been chosen for its biblical associations: with Joseph, the husband of the Virgin Mary; and beyond him, with Joseph, eleventh son of Jacob, the eponymous ancestor of Israel.

Even outside communities of faith, the story of that Joseph (found in Gen. 37 – 50) is known, rehearsed and valued. The official website for Andrew Lloyd Webber's famous musical, 'Joseph and his Technicolour Dreamcoat' estimates that almost forty years after its inaugural production in 1969, the show is still being performed in about 500 UK schools each year. So this story has a broad appeal.

But it is particularly a text for today. In many parts of the world (certainly in Western Europe and in the USA), the Christian Church is facing a double crisis: a crisis of decline on the one hand; and a crisis of disunity on the other.

The crisis of decline is, for many denominations, an attendance crisis and a financial one. The number of people attending public worship in Britain, for example, has been falling for decades, and despite some encouraging signs (individual congregations bucking the trend, especially in suburban areas; 'fresh expressions' of church promoting new opportunities for worship, especially midweek), the evidence does not yet suggest the pattern has been reversed. This attendance crisis is often compounded by a financial one: not least because of an increasing pensions' burden, shrinking congregations are being asked to meet costs (relating chiefly to the provision of stipendiary ministries) which are rising sharply year by year. Most Dioceses in the Church of England, for example, are in acute difficulty balancing the books; and the situation is not much different in other historic denominations. Since 1980, the percentage of the population affirming allegiance to any church denomination has dropped more than 20% in Belgium, 18% in the Netherlands and 16% in France. Across Europe as a whole, the number of people who identify themselves as Roman Catholic – by far the biggest denomination on the Continent – has fallen by more than a third since 1978.

In addition there is a crisis of 'disunity', relating to controversies especially over the place of women in ordained ministries and the place of practising homosexuals within the church.

If there was ever a time when the two aspects of this double crisis (the decline on the one hand and the disunity on the other) were separate, that day is long gone. Generally speaking, in Britain, the congregations which have been most effective evangelistically in the last ten years and have defied the trend of decline, have also been highly effective in encouraging the discipline of tithing among their members making such churches centres of wealth. On the whole, these same churches tend to be charismatic and evangelical in style and so tend to adopt conservative, traditional stances in relation to the issue of both women in leadership and homosexuality. In the USA and Africa, of course, the polarization of wealth, growth and conservatism on the one hand and poverty, decline and liberalism does not exist: but in those parts of the world too, wealth, growth and theological stance are thoroughly intertwined.

The church needs always to be hearing and responding to the Word of the Lord. In a time of crisis that need is most urgent. In seeking to respond faithfully to God in the face of decline and disunity, the church is bound to attend carefully to what the Lord is saying. But where is the Word of God to be heard?

It can be heard in the story of Joseph. There are obvious reasons for this. For one thing, the story of Joseph is about living faithfully in the face of adversity. In the first half of the story, the adversity is a personal one: Joseph is wronged by his own brothers and then by Potiphar and his wife. Later in the story, the adversity is a social one: not just Joseph's family, but all the world, faces famine and starvation.

There are good grounds to suppose that a church in the midst of adversity may find encouragement and inspiration and may hear the Word of the Lord in a story set in a time of adversity. Moreover, in adversity, Joseph wrestles with the issues of money, sex and power. These are just the issues over which the church finds itself in controversy today. Of course, these issues have always represented a kind of unholy trinity for Christian disciples, which is why nuns and monks have traditionally taken vows of poverty, chastity and obedience. But it is the context of adversity that makes the story of Joseph a promising place within the tradition for the contemporary church in the West to turn as it seeks to live out the will of God.

Secondly, the story of Joseph is a story about the costly experience of forgiveness and reconciliation. In the decisive act of the story, Joseph is sold into slavery in Egypt by his brothers in Canaan. The story makes it clear that this was an atrocious thing for his brothers to do to him. But it also makes it plain that Joseph himself was no saint and to some extent provoked their hostility. The story portrays the maturing of Joseph and his brothers in the face of the adversities that beset them, so that they can be truly reconciled. An important and neglected feature of the story is the fact that although Joseph and his brothers are superficially reconciled about half way through the narrative (in Gen. 42), it is not until the very end of the story (in Gen. 50) that the reconciliation is complete. After seven chapters, their reunion is only physical; it is another seven chapters before it becomes something profoundly emotional.

There are also good grounds then to suppose that a church in the midst of disunity may find encouragement and inspiration and may hear the Word of the Lord in a story in which trust is not rebuilt between the estranged parties overnight. Part of the challenge facing the church is how to maintain relationships which are strained and how to repair those that are broken. The church faces this challenge locally, nationally and globally. Again, the story of Joseph is a promising place in the tradition for the contemporary church to turn as it seeks to live out the will of God when its relationships are strained and broken.

The Joseph Story: A Drama in Fourteen Episodes

The Joseph story is sometimes described by scholars as 'the Joseph cycle'. This is a helpful term. In Genesis, there are similarly 'cycles' of stories about Abraham (Gen. 12 – 25) and Jacob (Gen. 26 – 36); and in other parts of the Bible, there is a 'David Cycle' for example (1 Sam. 16 – 1 Kgs. 2) and one about Elijah (1 Kgs. 17 – 2 Kgs. 2). A 'cycle' in this sense is a series of connected and continuous narratives about a central figure, in which the component parts nevertheless have their own separate coherence and integrity – like episodes in a TV drama series perhaps or like the individual parts in a 'cycle' of Medieval Mystery Plays.

It is on this understanding that the Joseph story is approached in the chapters that follow. Each 'episode' is treated as a drama in its own right, made up often of several distinct 'scenes'; but with due attention to its place in the unfolding of the narrative as a whole. The narrative sequence and chronology are respected – and interrogated for meaning.

Often, but not always, a chapter in this book corresponds to a chapter of the biblical text. In each chapter special effort has been made to follow the contours of the Bible passage, attending carefully to its shape and structure. The text has been read realistically, attending to the literary details in the story. Like a novel, this text has to be taken at face value, to some extent, if its meaning is to be appropriated. There has been a certain amount of reading between the lines of the text, but always with the aim of enabling the narrative to have its full dramatic impact.

To assist in this task, the biblical text, divided up into 'episodes' and 'scenes', is printed together with the commentary. The translation is the *New Revised Standard Version* – chosen for the balance it achieves between a closeness to the Hebrew text on the one hand, and a fluency of contemporary English on the other.

But what is offered here is also 'a theological exposition' – and to be specific, a Christian theological exposition. This does not mean that in the following chapters every opportunity has been taken to draw parallels between Joseph and Jesus. There is a long tradition of this kind of 'typology' in the church. The aim in this book has been a little different. This book asks what the Word of the Lord might be to the contemporary church through this story, and attempts to answer that question 'in the light of Christ'. What do we learn from this text, in other words, given the nature of God as he has made himself known in Jesus Christ?

There is little here, therefore, in the way of interaction with other interpreters of the text (there are no footnotes) or with current academic scholarship. During the last two hundred years or more much has been written about the development of this text as part of the book of Genesis. It is clear that the text has a history: it took shape over time, almost certainly at first in an oral culture as a spoken tale. It wasn't written in a single sitting by a single author. But the form it now has it has had for at least two thousand years, and what is offered here is a reading of *this* text in *this* form. Readers wishing to pursue questions of source criticism should turn to the standard commentaries. In particular, where this book comments on the Hebrew text, its observations are derived from the insights of others.

In my own reading of the story, I have been especially helped by the interpretations of John Calvin, Claus Westermann, R.S. Wallace, R.T. Kendall, Robert Alter and Walter Brueggemann – and readers who know their work will doubtless discern my indebtedness, which I am glad to acknowledge. I have also been greatly assisted by the opportunity to work through the story twice in Bible study and sermon series at St. Paul's Church at The Crossing in Walsall, and I have benefitted from the perception of members of the congregation there. It is to them that this book is dedicated, with a thankful heart.

Thanks also to Jonathan and Tom for encouraging me to 'do Bible reading', and to Cathy for encouraging me to write – as if one writer in the family was not enough.

Pete Wilcox,
Lichfield Cathedral
Epiphany 2007

Chapter One

'Here comes this dreamer'

(Genesis 37)

Introduction

The story of Joseph starts as it means to go on: without any mention of God. That is not strictly true, of course: although there really isn't any reference to God or 'the Lord' in Genesis 37, there is in almost every other chapter of Genesis 38 – 50 (Chapter 47 is the other exception). And yet in the drama of the Joseph story God is never quite centre stage. It's clear that God is at work as the story unfolds, steering it to its intended conclusion; but his hand is hidden and his voice is usually only heard offstage. He is only once said to speak or to act directly (when he speaks to Jacob in a vision in Chapter 46). As a rule, in this part of Scripture, those who trust in God do so despite a dearth of encouragement to do so. This is part of the great value of the story of Joseph for the church today. There is a tendency in some contemporary church circles to expect the hand of God to be prominent – as it was in the life of Abraham, to whom God spoke and appeared repeatedly. Among Christian disciples today miracles are sought daily, answers to prayer anticipated keenly, and gifts of the Spirit celebrated rapturously. But for many believers dramatic experiences of the presence of God are the precious exception rather than the rule. Mostly, God acts in hidden ways. His purpose is mostly evident in retrospect. The life of faith mostly involves trust in a presence of God, which is elusive.

On the face of it, then, the first episode in the drama of Joseph's story unfolds without reference to God. As the story unfolds, however, it is clear God is present and very much at work. This 'absent presence' of God is characteristic of the whole narrative.

Episode One of the Joseph story (Gen. 37) has two scenes: in the first, set in the family home, Jacob is a key figure. In the biblical text of this chapter and of Chapters 42 – 50, the names Jacob and Israel are used interchangeably and apparently randomly; the same is true in the commentary. The Joseph story is introduced as 'the story of the family of Jacob.' It is a dysfunctional family. The first scene introduces us to Joseph the dreamer in his brash youthfulness (verses 1–11) and to the strain in his relationship with his brothers. In scene two (verses 12–36), Jacob (like God) is crucially absent. Scene two takes place away from the family home, where Joseph's brothers are tending the flock and seize the opportunity to rid themselves of their hated brother.

Scene One: Joseph and his Dreams (verses 1–11)

1 Jacob settled in the land where his father had lived as an alien, the land of Canaan. 2 This is the story of the family of Jacob.

Joseph, being seventeen years old, was shepherding the flock with his brothers; he was a helper to the sons of Bilhah and Zilpah, his father's wives; and Joseph brought a bad report of them to their father. 3 Now Israel loved Joseph more than any other of his children, because he was the son of his old age; and he had made him a long robe with sleeves. 4 But when his brothers saw that their father loved him more than all his brothers, they hated him, and could not speak peaceably to him.

5 Once Joseph had a dream, and when he told it to his brothers, they hated him even more. 6 He said to them, 'Listen to this dream that I dreamed. 7 There we were, binding sheaves in the field. Suddenly my sheaf rose and stood upright; then your sheaves gathered around it, and bowed down to my sheaf.' 8 His brothers said to him, 'Are you indeed to reign over us? Are you indeed to have dominion over us?' So they hated him even more because of his dreams and his words. 9 He had another dream, and told it to his brothers, saying, 'Look, I have had another dream: the sun, the moon, and eleven stars were bowing down to me.' 10 But when he told it to his father and to his brothers, his father rebuked him, and

said to him, 'What kind of dream is this that you have had? Shall we indeed come, I and your mother and your brothers, and bow to the ground before you?' 11 So his brothers were jealous of him, but his father kept the matter in mind.

In scene one, Joseph is shepherding the family flock with his brothers. It is striking that in scene two, he is not. We are not told why, although it seems likely that it is the direct result of what happens in scene one.

Joseph is seventeen: an adult, but not a mature man. Old enough to shepherd the flock with his brothers, he is also young enough still to be 'a helper' to the sons of two of his father's four wives, Bilhah and Zilpah. He is a youth for whom the future lies open; and he is his father's favourite. We are told that 'Israel loved Joseph more than any other of his children, because he was the son of his old age' (verse 3); but readers of the earlier part of the Jacob story know this is only half the truth. Israel really loved Joseph because he was the firstborn son of his favourite wife, Rachel (Gen. 29:30; 30:22–24); and Israel himself had been a favourite child, at least to his mother (Gen. 25:28).

Israel's favouritism of Joseph was not a discreet and closet thing: it was flaunted. He had made Joseph a special robe (whether a 'coat of many colours' or one with long sleeves; the same word is used to describe the coat worn by Tamar in 2 Sam. 13:18). His father's favouritism undoubtedly fuelled the hatred of his brothers towards Joseph; but so did his own behaviour: he used to speak ill of them to him. One way or another, the outcome was a falling out: Joseph was increasingly estranged from his brothers. They 'hated him and could not speak peaceably to him' (verse 4).

Commentators sometimes take pains to excuse Joseph: it was not his fault that his father favoured him; and if his brothers behaved badly, it was Joseph's duty to report them. But we are not in fact told that the brothers behaved badly – only that Joseph gave a bad report of them to his father. The impression is of a telltale: what Joseph knew about his brothers he might have stewarded more wisely. No doubt Jacob must take responsibility for his poor parenting: a parent who spoils a child is always acting in his or her own interests, not those of the child – and the outcome

will ultimately almost always be misery for the child. But the text
does not invite us to exonerate Joseph; on the contrary, it invites
us to see Joseph, as the curtain rises on his story, as a spoiled and
arrogant individual. He is a brat. Yet it is this Joseph, the flawed
and muddled individual, who (sometimes inadvertently) proves
to be the recipient and the instrument of God's grace. That is part
of the point of the story.

This deteriorating situation is compounded by Joseph's
dreams. It is implied, though not stated, that his dreams came
from God. They were the gift of the Holy Spirit. But, as many a
local congregation in the church today has discovered, the fact
that a person has a gift from God is no guarantee that they also
have the wisdom and maturity to use it well. On the contrary,
God's gifts are frequently abused by those to whom they are
given; it is characteristic of the grace of God that the gifts are not
therefore retracted.

Joseph dreamt, firstly, of sheaves in a field: his own and his
brothers'. Lo and behold, his brothers' sheaves bowed down to
his own. We are not told whether Joseph thought twice before
sharing this dream with them. Given the estrangement growing
between them, it is hard to imagine there wasn't an element of
gloating – or at least an overwhelming self-preoccupation – in his
relating of the dream. The outcome was not surprising: his brothers hated him even more (verse 5). In case we miss the point, it is
repeated: when he told them the dream, they hated him even
more (verse 8). There is a mounting intensity in these three references to the brothers' hatred for Joseph.

At this stage in his life, at least in this aspect of life, Joseph was
not a quick learner. He had another dream, of the sun and moon
and eleven stars bowing down to him. This time Joseph shared it
not only with his brothers, but with his father as well, so that his
father was moved – a rare event, this, for a spoiled child – to
rebuke him (verse 10). The rebuke is well deserved: the vision
Joseph experienced may well have come from God. It would,
broadly speaking, one day be fulfilled – although never quite so
completely and obviously as the first dream, not least because
Rachel, the 'moon', was by now already dead (Gen. 35:19).

Later in the story, Joseph will tell Pharaoh that the 'doubling of
[a] dream means that the thing is fixed by God, and God will

surely bring it about' (Gen. 41:32), and it is a fair assumption that here too the gift of two broadly similar dreams is a mark of their certain future fulfilment.

Joseph is a prophet then; but he is not the last recipient of a prompting of God's Spirit to prove such promptings can be handled in unspiritual and unedifying ways. Experiences of the Spirit are in themselves no mark of spiritual maturity; it is the wise and generous use of them which demonstrates the godliness of the believer.

The outcome is again predictable: 'his brothers were jealous of him.' 'But', we're told, 'his father kept the matter in mind' (verse 11). Christian readers will be reminded of Mary, who 'pondered in her heart' the prophecies made about her son (Lk. 2:19, compare 2:51). The 'but' in the text may be important: perhaps Jacob wanted the dream to come true, perhaps he wanted a special destiny for his favourite son, partly as a vindication of his favouritism.

Scene one ends where it begins – with Jacob. It is a reminder that 'the story of Joseph' is not about him alone, but about the people of God.

Scene Two: Joseph and his Brothers (verses 12–36)

> 12 Now his brothers went to pasture their father's flock near Shechem. 13 And Israel said to Joseph, 'Are not your brothers pasturing the flock at Shechem? Come, I will send you to them.' He answered, 'Here I am.' 14 So he said to him, 'Go now, see if it is well with your brothers and with the flock; and bring word back to me.' So he sent him from the valley of Hebron. He came to Shechem, 15 and a man found him wandering in the fields; the man asked him, 'What are you seeking?' 16 'I am seeking my brothers,' he said; 'tell me, please, where they are pasturing the flock.' 17 The man said, 'They have gone away, for I heard them say, "Let us go to Dothan."' So Joseph went after his brothers, and found them at Dothan. 18 They saw him from a distance, and before he came near to them, they conspired to kill him. 19 They said to one another, 'Here comes this dreamer. 20 Come now, let us kill him and throw him into one of the pits; then we shall say that a wild animal has

devoured him, and we shall see what will become of his dreams.'
21 But when Reuben heard it, he delivered him out of their hands,
saying, 'Let us not take his life.' 22 Reuben said to them, 'Shed no
blood; throw him into this pit here in the wilderness, but lay no
hand on him' – that he might rescue him out of their hand and
restore him to his father. 23 So when Joseph came to his brothers,
they stripped him of his robe, the long robe with sleeves that he
wore; 24 and they took him and threw him into a pit. The pit was
empty; there was no water in it. 25 Then they sat down to eat; and
looking up they saw a caravan of Ishmaelites coming from Gilead,
with their camels carrying gum, balm, and resin, on their way to
carry it down to Egypt. 26 Then Judah said to his brothers, 'What
profit is it if we kill our brother and conceal his blood? 27 Come, let
us sell him to the Ishmaelites, and not lay our hands on him, for he
is our brother, our own flesh.' And his brothers agreed. 28 When
some Midianite traders passed by, they drew Joseph up, lifting him
out of the pit, and sold him to the Ishmaelites for twenty pieces of
silver. And they took Joseph to Egypt. 29 When Reuben returned to
the pit and saw that Joseph was not in the pit, he tore his clothes.
30 He returned to his brothers, and said, 'The boy is gone; and I,
where can I turn?' 31 Then they took Joseph's robe, slaughtered a
goat, and dipped the robe in the blood. 32 They had the long robe
with sleeves taken to their father, and they said, 'This we have
found; see now whether it is your son's robe or not.' 33 He recog-
nized it, and said, 'It is my son's robe! A wild animal has devoured
him; Joseph is without doubt torn to pieces.' 34 Then Jacob tore his
garments, and put sackcloth on his loins, and mourned for his son
many days. 35 All his sons and all his daughters sought to comfort
him; but he refused to be comforted, and said, 'No, I shall go down
to Sheol to my son, mourning.' Thus his father bewailed him.
36 Meanwhile the Midianites had sold him in Egypt to Potiphar,
one of Pharaoh's officials, the captain of the guard.

Scene two follows after some unspecified interval. Unlike in
scene one, Joseph is no longer pasturing the flock with his brothers. But Jacob calls Joseph to run an errand, to visit his brothers
at Shechem and to bring word that they are safe and well (as the
boy David would later visit his older brothers on the field of bat-
tle, 1 Sam. 17:17–18).

Joseph's response is perhaps surprising for someone so spoiled. He says, 'Here I am.' These are the words of a faithful and diligent servant. They are used here for the seventh time in the book of Genesis. The same words have already been spoken by Abraham to God, when he was called by name in 22:1; by Abraham to Isaac when he was called 'Father' in 22:7; by Abraham to the angel of the Lord when he was called by name ('Abraham, Abraham') in 22:11; by Esau to Isaac when he was called 'My son!' in 27:1; by Isaac to Jacob when he was called 'Father' in 27:18; and by Jacob to the angel of the Lord when he was called by name in 31:11. The same words will be used again once more before the end of the book, by Jacob when he is called by name ('Jacob, Jacob') by God (in 46:2). The very same words are used by Moses in Exodus 3:4, when he is called by name by the Lord ('Moses, Moses'); repeatedly by Samuel in 1 Samuel 3:4, 6,8,16, when he is called by the Lord (though the boy believes it is Eli calling); by the priest Ahimelech when he is called by name by Saul in 1 Samuel 22:12; and in the New Testament by Ananias, when he is called by name by the Lord in Acts 9:10. The words are always a response to an intimate personal summons and they imply a prompt readiness to obey: 'Here I am, ready and waiting for your instructions;' 'Here I am, at your service.'

They are good and appropriate words for Joseph to use – if a little surprising to hear on the lips of a spoilt teenager (and if, as these references suggest, they really are the words of a faithful servant, they are still more startling to hear on the lips of the Almighty in response to his people when they call on him by name. But this is how they are used in Isaiah 58:9 and 65:1).

The words are also surprising, because Joseph already knows (verse 13) what it is his father is asking of him. He knows that to do what is being asked of him will mean leaving the comfortable atmosphere of a home in which he is preferred, for the hostility of his brothers' company; and it will mean a long and potentially hazardous journey. Shechem, to which his brothers had gone, was not a gentle stroll from the valley of Hebron where Joseph had remained at the family home. It was a distance of about 60 miles – a three or four day hike.

When Joseph reached Shechem, there was no sign of his brothers (verse 14). Eventually a stranger came across him wandering aimlessly in the field, and asked if he could help. Joseph requested directions to his brothers and was told that they had gone on to Dothan. If Dothan is to be identified with modern-day Tell Dotha, it is another twenty miles further north again – another day's hiking at least. The reader might have understood if Joseph had given up on his errand at this point, to return home. But he persevered and eventually caught up with his brothers there.

They saw and recognised him from a distance. [For Christian readers, the moment stands in stark contrast to the response of the compassionate father, when he saw and recognised, also from a distance, his prodigal son in Jesus' parable (Lk. 15:11–32)]. When they saw him they not only recognised him (at least partly on account of the coat he was wearing, to which there is emphatic reference in verse 23), they also recognised his vulnerability. Just for once, it was Joseph and his brothers (the cast of the first dream): Joseph without the protection of Jacob. So they resolved to kill him. 'Here comes the dreamer,' they said (literally, in Hebrew, *'the lord of dreams'*).

Evidently, Joseph's dreams had got to his brothers. It wasn't the coat that galled them now, but the dreams. They thought that if they snuffed out the dreamer, they would snuff out the power of the dream to determine the future. Whether they sensed that their hostility to Joseph was in any sense a hostility to the God who inspired the dreams isn't clear – perhaps it was just a hostility to that part of Joseph's character that was least worthy of God.

'Let's kill him', they said to one another. 'We can say that a wild animal has devoured him. Then we'll see what will become of his dreams' (verse 20). But the oldest brother, Reuben, was not so sure. He intervened in an attempt to deliver his brother. 'Let's not kill him,' he said. Perhaps, as his oldest son, he felt the greatest responsibility to his father. On the other hand, his past record was not of unswerving loyalty to Jacob. He had at some point had sex with Bilhah, one of his father's wives (Gen. 35:22).

If Reuben's intention was to 'rescue him out of the brothers' hand and restore him to his father', his intervention was not urgent or decisive enough. When Joseph reached his brothers, they stripped him of his coat and threw him into a dry pit. Then, callously, they sat down to eat – presumably laughing and joking their way through the meal, against the background of Joseph's shouts of protest. Looking up, they saw a trading caravan of Ishmaelites (or Midianites) coming down from Gilead (north of Shechem), bound for Egypt. It's not clear why the traders are identified alternately as Ishmaelites (verses 25,27,28) and Midianites (verse 28). Some scholars detect alternative sources behind the Joseph story here, rival threads which have been woven together into the story's present shape. But clearly the conflict was not sufficient to trouble any editor responsible for giving the story its present form, and the simplest explanation (that the two terms were in some way synonymous) may be the best – a solution supported by Judges 8:24. On the other hand, there is certainly something of an anachronism here: there has hardly been time for Ishmael – Joseph's great uncle – to establish a tribe in his name, let alone one which has become synonymous with Midian; and the wording in verse 28 especially does appear to imply two different groups of people.

At any event, the approach of the traders prompted qualms in a second brother, about the wisdom of the brothers' plan. This time it was Judah's turn to have misgivings, although it's possible his alternative plan was motivated more by the prospect of financial gain, than by compassion for Joseph (later in the story – in Genesis 42 – 44 – it will again be Reuben and Judah who stand out among the brothers as the leaders and decision makers). 'What profit is there', he asks ambiguously, 'if we kill our brother and conceal his blood?' His brothers (minus Reuben, who is absent at the crucial moment) readily agree, and they sell him for twenty pieces of silver. For Christian readers, the sense of betrayal is heightened by the reference to pieces of silver (compare Mt. 26:15 and its parallels).

Joseph disappears from his brothers' sight in the company of the traders, not to be seen by them again for twenty two years. When Reuben returns, it is too late. He tears his clothes in anguish, focused at once on the implications for their return home. Together the brothers devise their story: they never saw Joseph; he never found them; they just happened to stumble across his coat, covered in blood, and surmised the rest.

They return home. Whether Jacob was watching for his favourite son to return, we are not told. The other brothers show their father the bloodied coat and let him reach the obvious conclusion: 'It is my son's robe.' The phrase may be exclusive, as if Jacob has only one son, or only one son that truly matters. If so, and if the brothers had any twinges of conscience in their father's presence, that remark smothered them. 'A wild animal has devoured him,' Jacob concludes. 'Joseph is without doubt torn to pieces' (verse 33).

The brothers thought Joseph's removal from the scene would improve matters at home. But they were mistaken. One after another, they – and their sisters (making a rare and welcome intrusion into a relentlessly male narrative) – tried to comfort their father. But Jacob (making his last appearance in the story until Chapter 46) refused. He made up his mind – faithlessly, it has to be said – to go down to his grave in mourning. He will wear black until the day he dies. More might have been expected from the man who wrestled with God at Peniel (in Gen. 32:22–32), or knew his blessing at Bethel (in Gen. 35:9–15). But Jacob was born tenacious (Gen. 25:26) and now clings stubbornly to his grief.

Joseph, 'meanwhile' (see verse 36; this is another loaded word in this story), was taken down to Egypt. Traders travelling from Shechem to Egypt must inevitably have passed close to, if not in fact through, Joseph's home territory of Hebron. Perhaps at some stage on the journey he harboured thoughts of a speedy escape and return home, and a speedy fulfilment of the dreams he had dreamt. Often though, the purposes of God are not fulfilled either speedily or easily. It is a fantasy to expect otherwise.

Chapter Two

'She is more in the right than I'

(Genesis 38)

Introduction

Commentators and preachers expounding the Joseph story frequently omit Genesis 38. Presumably this has less to do with its unsavoury content, than with the fact that on the face of it the chapter is an excursus or digression. It seems to have little to do with Joseph. He is not mentioned at all and the narrative about him is not obviously advanced. Chapter 38 is so disconnected from the flow of Chapters 37 and 39, in fact, that an editor might easily have placed it not in its present position, but after Chapter 36. In such a case, or if Genesis 38 were omitted altogether, would the Joseph story be impoverished?

Perhaps it would. Presumably the hand that gave the book of Genesis the shape in which it has come to us had some purpose in placing it where it is. The very fact that this story about Judah jars, and feels like an abrupt interruption, should alert a sensitive reader to its significance in the whole scheme. If it was irrelevant, why was it retained in such an apparently awkward and inappropriate place?

There are two reasons. The first has to do with Judah. Of all the brothers, he plays the most prominent part in the Joseph drama. Although he is only the fourth son of Jacob, he is far more prominent than Simeon and Levi. He is more prominent even than Reuben, the oldest, who (more predictably) does also play a leading role. Judah's brief intervention in Chapter 37 is followed by more significant contributions to the unfolding story in Chapters

43 (verses 3–10), 44 (verses 14–34) and 46 (verse 28). And in the great 'blessing' spoken by Jacob to his sons in Chapter 49, the words addressed to Judah (verses 8–12) occupy more space than those addressed to any other brother but Joseph (verses 22–26). The development in the character of Joseph over the course of the whole narrative is hard to miss: it charts his growth towards maturity as a human being. Perhaps this present episode is included to provide readers with an insight into the development and growth of Judah too. In particular, his sin and repentance in this chapter paves the way for his great speech in Chapter 44.

Secondly, the interlude in the Joseph story is itself important. He has been taken away to a far country. Dramatically it is appropriate for a distance to be created between the chilling last words of Chapter 37 verse 28 ('They took Joseph to Egypt') and the first lines of Chapter 39 ('Now Joseph was taken down to Egypt, and Potiphar . . . an Egyptian, bought him from the Ishmaelites . . .'): it serves to let suspense grow and to develop the sense that Joseph has been forgotten.

There are also significant literary links between this chapter and those on either side of it, as we shall see. So this episode has an appropriate place in an exposition of the Joseph cycle.

Genesis 38 falls into three parts. The drama unfolds in three scenes. The real action of the story, in which Tamar tricks her father in law Judah into having sex with her and conceives his child, takes place in scene two, in verses 12–23. Scene one (the first eleven verses) tells us what happened in the years that led up to that day, and the third scene (the final seven verses, from verse 24 onwards), provides the denouement and tells us what happened in the months that followed it.

Scene One: The Background (verses 1–11)

> 1 It happened at that time that Judah went down from his brothers and settled near a certain Adullamite whose name was Hirah. 2 There Judah saw the daughter of a certain Canaanite whose name was Shua; he married her and went in to her. 3 She conceived and bore a son; and he named him Er. 4 Again she conceived and bore a son whom she named Onan. 5 Yet again she

bore a son, and she named him Shelah. She was in Chezib when she bore him. 6 Judah took a wife for Er his firstborn; her name was Tamar. 7 But Er, Judah's firstborn, was wicked in the sight of the LORD, and the LORD put him to death. 8 Then Judah said to Onan, 'Go in to your brother's wife and perform the duty of a brother-in-law to her; raise up offspring for your brother.' 9 But since Onan knew that the offspring would not be his, he spilled his semen on the ground whenever he went in to his brother's wife, so that he would not give offspring to his brother. 10 What he did was displeasing in the sight of the LORD, and he put him to death also. 11 Then Judah said to his daughter-in-law Tamar, 'Remain a widow in your father's house until my son Shelah grows up' – for he feared that he too would die, like his brothers. So Tamar went to live in her father's house.

Judah, the fourth of Jacob's twelve sons, had left the rest of his family to settle close to his friend, Hirah the Adullamite. How distant this was from his family, and how far it was a reaction to the events in Chapter 37, we are not told. Perhaps he could not bear to live in a house dominated by his father's grief. Perhaps Hiram was someone he had met pasturing the flocks near Shechem or Dothan. The text is silent on these points.

Having settled, Judah found a Canaanite wife, a daughter of Shua, who bore him three sons: Er, Onan and Shelah. Whether Judah's actions here are reported neutrally or with criticism is hard to gauge. It may be that the narrator regards both his voluntary separation from the rest of the family and his taking of a Canaanite wife as reprehensible; but if so, the point is not pressed. Judah's isolation from the rest of his family endures long enough for his oldest son, Er, to grow up. So Judah finds him a wife called Tamar (verse 6). But Er was wicked and 'the Lord put him to death'. Neither the nature of Er's wickedness nor the nature of God's judgment are elaborated. Judah then did what, as the head of the household, he was expected to do in that culture (at least, in the eyes of the shaper of Genesis): he gave the dead man's wife to his next son, Onan, so that Er's name should not die with him.

This custom (called 'levirate marriage', from the Latin word *levir*, meaning brother in law) was still in force, at least in theory, at the time of Jesus. Christian readers will recall the question with which the Sadducees came to him, about a woman who was married, in turn, to seven brothers, each of whom died: 'whose wife will she be in the resurrection?' (Mk. 12:19–23 and parallels). The law is set out formally in Deuteronomy 25:5–10.

But Onan didn't want offspring that wouldn't be regarded as his own, so he deliberately spilled his semen on the ground 'whenever he went in to his brother's wife' (verse 9). This is the episode which has given rise to the term (especially in traditional Roman Catholic teaching) 'Onanism'. As a method of contraception, *coitus interruptus* is notoriously unreliable; but in this situation it was apparently effective. Tamar was denied children, and the Lord, displeased, put Onan to death also.

The rather sinister verses 7 and 10 contain the first references to God in the Joseph story. The phrase 'the Lord put him to death' is shocking to modern ears. The shock is magnified both by the fact that it forms the reader's 'first impression' of God and by the fact that the narrator uses it so lightly. In terms of the narrative, the phrase is something of an aside. In one sense, it means little more than 'he died': the phrase assumes a worldview in which life and death are in the hands of God, and are directly attributed to him. Of any death, in other words, the narrator might have said that the deceased was 'put to death' by the Lord. But in another sense, the narrator is plainly making a judgment. Much is left unsaid, but the phrase implies 'his death is to be regarded as a punishment for his sin'. In terms of this episode, the phrase serves to alert the reader not to any capriciousness in God, but to the seriousness of the situation. After this opening scene, the reader knows that the stakes are high: the Lord regards the treatment of Tamar as heinous.

But Shelah, Judah's youngest son, was not yet old enough to be married, so Judah again did what he was supposed to do, and sent Tamar to live as a widow in her father's house, until Shelah grew up – implying that at that point she would be given to him in marriage. But in verse 11 we find that by now Judah was afraid. His two oldest sons have died young, and the common factor is Tamar. He's worried that she's some kind of black widow, a bringer of death, and he's got no intention of risking the loss of Shelah too. But Tamar is bound by Judah's word: she is not free to seek a husband outside Judah's family. So she returns to her father's house, to wait.

Scene Two: The Central Action (verses 12–23)

> 12 In course of time the wife of Judah, Shua's daughter, died; when Judah's time of mourning was over, he went up to Timnah to his sheepshearers, he and his friend Hirah the Adullamite. 13 When Tamar was told, 'Your father-in-law is going up to Timnah to shear his sheep,' 14 she put off her widow's garments, put on a veil, wrapped herself up, and sat down at the entrance to Enaim, which is on the road to Timnah. She saw that Shelah was grown up, yet she had not been given to him in marriage. 15 When Judah saw her, he thought her to be a prostitute, for she had covered her face. 16 He went over to her at the road side, and said, 'Come, let me come in to you,' for he did not know that she was his daughter-in-law. She said, 'What will you give me, that you may come in to me?' 17 He answered, 'I will send you a kid from the flock.' And she said, 'Only if you give me a pledge, until you send it.' 18 He said, 'What pledge shall I give you?' She replied, 'Your signet and your cord, and the staff that is in your hand.' So he gave them to her, and went in to her, and she conceived by him. 19 Then she got up and went away, and taking off her veil she put on the garments of her widowhood. 20 When Judah sent the kid by his friend the Adullamite, to recover the pledge from the woman, he could not find her. 21 He asked the townspeople, 'Where is the temple prostitute who was at Enaim by the wayside?' But they said, 'No prostitute has been here.' 22 So he returned to Judah, and said, 'I have not found her; moreover the townspeople said, "No prostitute has been here."' 23 Judah replied, 'Let her keep the things as her own, otherwise we will be laughed at; you see, I sent this kid, and you could not find her.'

Now comes the central action, some years later. The next to die is Judah's wife, the daughter of Shua. Then one day, after the time of mourning was over (note the contrast between the triply bereaved Judah who is able to move on from his grief, and the not-truly bereaved Jacob, who isn't), at sheep shearing time (which meant 'party time'; a traditional time of celebration and excess in Canaanite culture, with shrine prostitutes doing brisk business), Judah went off with his friend Hirah the Adullamite to inspect the flocks at a place called Timnar. Tamar is still in her father's house, still bound by her father in law's word; but now fully aware that Shelah, though old enough, is never going to be given to her in marriage. She hears of Judah's trip and takes matters into her own hands. In fact, the text states that Tamar 'was told' (verse 13) that her father in law was in Timnar, as if others were complicit with her in her plan. The action she took was drastic: but she was not the last woman in a patriarchal society to find it necessary to resort to dubious means to achieve legitimate ends. Judah was denying her what was her civil right: to become a mother in the family of her deceased husband. So she employs what power she has and sets out to exploit what weakness she can find in her father in law.

Tamar took off her widow's attire and instead 'put on a veil' (verse 14; the ancient Canaanite equivalent of a short skirt and thigh boots) and 'sat down at the entrance to Enaim' (the ancient Canaanite equivalent of a lamp-post on a street corner). Sure enough, along comes Judah. When he sees Tamar, he takes her to be not his daughter in law (since she had been banished to her own father's house, he may not have seen her for some years) but a shrine prostitute. Prostitutes have to be recognisable; otherwise they would not do business. Judah 'thought her to be a prostitute, because she had covered her face' (verse 15). He himself is wifeless now and, perhaps feeling needy, he propositions her (just as Joseph will be propositioned in the next chapter). They negotiate briefly over a price and then she, canny woman, asks for a pledge. Tamar is no fool: she has found Judah to be untrue to his word in major matters and from a demonstrably untrustworthy man, she seeks guarantees in a relatively minor one. She requests and he, foolishly, hands over some of his personal effects – roughly equivalent, it has been suggested, to a person's driving licence and credit cards today – his staff and his seal (worn on a necklace, hence the cord).

Then she goes home, to take up again the garments and role of her widowhood. And Judah, meanwhile, sends his friend the Adullamite to honour his pledge. Presumably Judah was feeling a touch guilty about all this, because he doesn't go himself to deliver the goat and collect his staff, but sends an intermediary. But there's a problem: not only can the woman not be found, but the locals say there's never been a shrine prostitute on that road. So Judah says, 'I don't want to be a laughing stock, let her keep what she's got' (verse 23). The speed with which Judah concedes defeat in his search for the woman is a further mark of his bad conscience. His fear of becoming a laughing stock is also worth noting. It is a particular kind of man, with a particular sense of his importance in the community, of his social standing and public *persona*, whose greatest fear is to be laughed at. And in Judah's case – if indeed Tamar had conspirators working with her – it's too late: one part of his community is already sniggering. There is a note of self-righteousness in his words, when he says, 'You see, I sent this goat-kid, but you could not find her': 'I did what I said, I am a man of my word; it's not my fault if she has not got what she was promised'. The bigger breach of trust lies always just below the surface.

Scene Three: The Aftermath (verses 24–30)

> 24 About three months later Judah was told, 'Your daughter-in-law Tamar has played the whore; moreover she is pregnant as a result of whoredom.' And Judah said, 'Bring her out, and let her be burned.' 25 As she was being brought out, she sent word to her father-in-law, 'It was the owner of these who made me pregnant.' And she said, 'Take note, please, whose these are, the signet and the cord and the staff.' 26 Then Judah acknowledged them and said, 'She is more in the right than I, since I did not give her to my son Shelah.' And he did not lie with her again. 27 When the time of her delivery came, there were twins in her womb. 28 While she was in labour, one put out a hand; and the midwife took and bound on his hand a crimson thread, saying, 'This one came out first.' 29 But just then he drew back his hand, and out came his brother; and she said, 'What a breach you have made for yourself!' Therefore he was named Perez. 30 Afterward his brother came out with the crimson thread on his hand; and he was named Zerah.

The sequel comes in the last seven verses. Three months later, Judah hears that Tamar is pregnant and guilty of prostitution. As head of the household, he is responsible for justice. 'Bring her out', he says, 'burn her to death'. 'She swells with conception; he swells with rage' as another writer has it. His response is as severe as it is swift: there is no thought for the unborn (twins, as it happens), and no question of hearing what Tamar might have to say in her defence. Whether Judah's own conscience gave a twinge or not as he passed judgment, we don't know. But before the sentence is carried out, Tamar gets a message to him: 'I *am* pregnant (it's true) by the man who owns this seal and staff. You don't recognise them, do you?' The link with the Joseph story is unambiguous here: at the end of Chapter 37, when the brothers had brought to their father the garment stained in blood, they had said to him, in just the same phrase in the Hebrew as the one Tamar uses here, 'You don't recognise it, do you?' Recognition is a recurring theme in the whole narrative. And Judah responds (with self-recognition) in the most profoundly penitent words: 'She is more righteous than I, since I did not give her to my son Shelah', he says. Christian theologians have always argued that the knowledge of God goes hand in hand with a true knowledge of oneself.

The text continues, 'And he did not lie with her again' (verse 26). Judah thus acknowledges explicitly that he had done wrong by denying Tamar her marriage to Shelah (the underlying and major issue), and implicitly that he had done wrong by lying with her (the surface issue but relatively minor one), by not doing so again. A recognition is also implied that he was wrong to pass judgment so hastily.

There is a sequel to the sequel. We are not told whether Tamar was finally given in marriage to Shelah. Perhaps now that she was pregnant there was no need. The story ends instead with an account of the birth of Perez and Zerah, twins like their grandfather Jacob.

Conclusion

Genesis 38 is a story about Judah, tucked away in the larger story of Joseph. But tucked away in the larger story of Judah is the

story of Tamar. And in the great drama of salvation which we call
the Bible, she too has her place.

The opening verses of Matthew Chapter 1 (the genealogy of
Jesus Christ) sound like a list of the great and the good in Israel,
a list of the giants and heroes of the Old Testament. This is the
noble line into which Jesus, the best of the great and the good, the
giant of giants and hero of heroes, is born: Abraham, Isaac, Jacob,
Judah, Boaz, Obed, Jesse, David. But that is not Matthew's point;
or at least, not entirely. For Matthew subtly introduces into that
list the names of five women: Tamar, Rahab, Ruth, Bathsheba and
Mary (verses 3,5,6 – though in fact Bathsheba is not named; she is
'the wife of Uriah the Hittite' – and 16). The first three were not
even Israelites – though each of them in their own way 'sought
refuge under the wings of the LORD, the God of Israel' (Ruth 2:12);
all five, by the standards of their day, were in one way or another
disreputable. And yet by the grace of God, they've been woven
into Jesus' line: their stories have become part of the story of the
coming of God's kingdom. Of course, on closer inspection, the
men turn out to be less than giants and less than noble. They turn
out to be, if anything, still more disreputable and shady than the
five women. The list includes murderers, assassins, adulterers and
cheats. But they are none the less fully recipients of the grace of
God for that. That, surely, is Matthew's point.

By the end of the chapter, Judah has turned a corner: having separated from his family and taken a Canaanite wife, having
wronged his daughter in law and abused his position as the head
of the household in two, if not three, ways, he has come to a point
at which he is able to recognise his own shortcomings. It is a short
step, for Judah, from Genesis 38:26 ('She is more righteous than I
am') to Genesis 44:16 ('God has uncovered our guilt'). And yet, it
is a significant step, because God has yet to be named in this story.
It is not that God is absent or redundant in Chapters 37 and 38; but
it is significant for the meaning of the story that his role is not
acknowledged. In Genesis 37 – 38, if God is at work, bringing order
out of the chaos of Jacob's family life, or Judah's, that fact has to be
inferred. None of the cast of human characters has any idea, it
appears, at this stage in the drama, that this might be so: not Jacob
(despite his prior experience of God), not Joseph (despite his
dreams), and certainly not Judah or the Canaanite Tamar.

Chapter Three

'The Lord was with Joseph'

(Genesis 39)

Introduction

How do you tell when the Lord is 'with' someone? What are the marks of God's presence and blessing? The Church, and individual Christians, can be extraordinarily worldly in making judgments of this kind. In assessing the value of an evangelistic event, for example, or the effectiveness of a preacher, a church, or a ministry, we tend to ask, 'How big? How many?' – as if numbers mean success and as if 'success' is an infallible guide to the blessing and presence of God. This is, of course, a particular temptation in times of adversity. When church attendances are declining and finances are under pressure, it is so easy to conclude that the Spirit of God is most active where congregations are big, or wealthy, or at least growing. But such outward marks can be misleading. It is at least true that the absence of success is not necessarily equivalent to the absence of God.

Joseph's life, like most lives, was a rollercoaster ride: its ups and downs and twists and turns were perhaps more extreme than most, but the pattern he experienced is common enough. He must have been tempted to assume, not just that when things went well it was because the Lord was with him, but that when things went badly it was because the Lord had withdrawn his blessing. But although the text does indeed attribute Joseph's success to the Lord's presence with him, it emphatically does not say that when things went wrong for him, it was because the Lord was at a distance. There is no 'equals sign' in the life of faith as it is presented in the Bible, between material success on the one hand and the blessing of God on the other. It is true that passages of the Bible, not least in Deuteronomy (e.g., 28:1–14) and in the Psalms (e.g., Ps. 1:3), state that those who keep God's law will prosper. But by the same token, significant passages in the New Testament state bluntly that suffering and hardship are an inescapable part of the Christian life (especially 2 Corinthians and 1 Peter, but also, for example, 2 Tim. 3:12). To the Psalmist it seems all too often that it is the wicked, not the righteous, who prosper (e.g., Ps. 10:5).

The episode of the Joseph story related in Chapter 39 again falls into three scenes. The first and third scenes (verses 1–6a and 21–23) are parallel to each other. Both are short relative to the middle scene, which is far longer. In both scenes one and three, we meet the phrase 'the Lord was with Joseph' (verses 2,21,23); and in both, the Lord is said to make Joseph prosper (verses 3,23). In the second scene, by contrast, the Lord is, on the face of it, absent. To put it plainly: references to the Lord are concentrated in the first and third scenes: there are five references to the Lord in verses 1–6a and three in verses 21–23, but none at all in verses 6b–20. And yet the careful reader is in no doubt that the hand of the Lord is just as much on Joseph's life (perhaps more than ever) as the encouraging developments of Joseph's early months in Egypt give way to renewed adversity and trial. (When an English Bible says 'the LORD', in capital letters, it is in place of the Hebrew word YHWH, the special name by which God revealed himself to the Israelites; compare Gen. 4:26, Ex. 3:15; 33:19. In this book, 'the Lord' has been preferred simply as less clumsy on the reader's eye).

Scene One: A Turn for the Better (The Lord is Present, verses 1–6a)

1 Now Joseph was taken down to Egypt, and Potiphar, an officer of Pharaoh, the captain of the guard, an Egyptian, bought him from the Ishmaelites who had brought him down there. 2 The LORD was with Joseph, and he became a successful man; he was in the house of his Egyptian master. 3 His master saw that the LORD

was with him, and that the LORD caused all that he did to prosper in his hands. 4 So Joseph found favour in his sight and attended him; he made him overseer of his house and put him in charge of all that he had. 5 From the time that he made him overseer in his house and over all that he had, the LORD blessed the Egyptian's house for Joseph's sake; the blessing of the LORD was on all that he had, in house and field. 6 So he left all that he had in Joseph's charge; and, with him there, he had no concern for anything but the food that he ate.

The interlude of Chapter 38 enables the reader to enter into Joseph's transition from Canaan to Egypt: he left the stage at Genesis 37:28, sold into the hands of Ishmaelite traders; he reappears on stage at the start of Chapter 39, sold into the hands of Potiphar, 'an officer of Pharaoh, the captain of the guard, an Egyptian' (the fact is noted in an 'offstage aside' at Gen. 37:36). At this point, Joseph's future was still open: it might have unfolded from that point in a number of ways, although few of them can have been very hopeful. But 'the Lord was with Joseph and he became a successful man . . . The Lord caused all that he did to prosper in his hands' (verses 2–3). In fact, of course, the Lord had been with Joseph in Canaan – but it was only in adversity that Joseph learned to recognise the presence of God, and only in his subsequent prosperity that he grew to understand its source.

And it was not only Joseph to whom the Lord's presence became something recognisable. Joseph was so successful that Potiphar also acknowledged that it was the Lord's doing. This is in fact not completely unheard of either in the Joseph story or in the book of Genesis as a whole but it still commands our attention – the Lord's work is acknowledged by someone outside the family of Abraham. Potiphar was a discerning man and a shrewd one – when he saw Joseph's success and understood its source, he entrusted his house and estate to him: 'he made him overseer in his house and over all that he had' (verse 4).

The Lord in turn blessed Potiphar 'for Joseph's sake': 'the blessing of the Lord was on all that he had, in house and field' (verse 5). We shall see later in the story that 'blessing' is a particular theme in the book of Genesis, and indeed that the whole point of God choosing and blessing the family of Abraham by his grace was so that blessing might spread to all the nations of the earth – of whom Potiphar is here an early representative. This blessing in turn encouraged Potiphar to leave all his concerns in Joseph's hands. He didn't worry about anything except the food that he ate. It must have seemed to Joseph as if, against all the odds, life was sweet indeed. The narrative does not indicate how long this initial period of prosperity continued, but if Joseph was thirty years old when he later entered the service of Pharaoh (Gen. 41:46), and only two of those years passed after the incident in jail involving Pharaoh's cupbearer and baker (Gen. 41:1), then taken together, his time in jail and his time in Potiphar's house lasted eleven years. So we can probably measure this initial period in years, not months.

Scene Two: A Turn for the Worse (Is the Lord Absent? verses 6b–20)

> 6b Now Joseph was handsome and good-looking. 7 And after a time his master's wife cast her eyes on Joseph and said, 'Lie with me.' 8 But he refused and said to his master's wife, 'Look, with me here, my master has no concern about anything in the house, and he has put everything that he has in my hand. 9 He is not greater in this house than I am, nor has he kept back anything from me except yourself, because you are his wife. How then could I do this great wickedness, and sin against God?' 10 And although she spoke to Joseph day after day, he would not consent to lie beside her or to be with her. 11 One day, however, when he went into the house to do his work, and while no one else was in the house, 12 she caught hold of his garment, saying, 'Lie with me!' But he left his garment in her hand, and fled and ran outside. 13 When she saw that he had left his garment in her hand and had fled outside, 14 she called out to the members of her household and said to them, 'See, my husband has brought among us a Hebrew to insult us! He came in to me to lie with me, and I cried out with a loud voice; 15 and when he heard me raise my voice and cry out, he left his garment beside me, and fled outside.' 16 Then she kept his garment by her until his master came home, 17 and she told him the same story, saying, 'The Hebrew servant, whom you have

brought among us, came in to me to insult me; 18 but as soon as I raised my voice and cried out, he left his garment beside me, and fled outside.' 19 When his master heard the words that his wife spoke to him, saying, 'This is the way your servant treated me,' he became enraged. 20 And Joseph's master took him and put him into the prison, the place where the king's prisoners were confined; he remained there in prison.

It can reasonably be assumed therefore that Joseph was in his early twenties when his master's wife began to make passes at her husband's well-built and good-looking senior servant (exactly the same words used here to describe Joseph's good looks are used to describe his mother Rachel in Gen. 29:17). He was almost certainly a man of marriageable age, with sexual desires and needs of his own. However, his response (in verse 8) to what was not just a single regrettable lapse on the part of Potiphar's wife but a settled policy, a pattern of behaviour (sexual harassment, in fact, in the workplace), was admirable. This is only the fourth time in the narrative in which Joseph is said to speak; but already it is possible to discern a change. Joseph has grown through his trials.

Temptation, perhaps especially to sexual sin, can be as strong in times of ease and power as it is in times of stress and adversity – as King David found (2 Sam. 11:1–2). To judge from the recent record of many politicians, it seems that powerful and successful men (and within obvious limits, Joseph was powerful and successful) are especially vulnerable to advances of this kind. But Joseph finds the resources to resist the overtures of his master's wife. Her demand is expressed in just two words in Hebrew; an Anglo-Saxon equivalent is not hard to think of. Joseph's response is far longer and his words demonstrate that ultimately the resources he finds are derived from God. For the first time in the narrative, Joseph is presented as a man of faith. His conscience will not permit him to accept the woman's proposition because to do so would be to dishonour first Potiphar, who has trusted him ('he has put everything that he has in my hand . . .'); second, Potiphar's wife herself ('he has not kept anything back from me except yourself, because you are his wife' . . .); and third, ultimately, God ('how then could I do this great wickedness and sin against God?'). His response is not to say, 'What if we get caught? I have too much to lose', or 'No thanks, you're not my type', but 'How could I offend God in such a way?' This is the first time in the story that Joseph has made a confession of faith. His words imply not just certain convictions about God, but a relationship with God. It is out of an appropriate intimacy with the Lord that Joseph is able to refuse an inappropriate intimacy with the woman.

Like Judah before him (Gen. 38:26), Joseph follows up his words with a change in his behaviour: although she pestered him day after day, he refused not just to sleep with her, but even to be with her. Persistent temptation is often best dealt with by building fences around fences in this way.

But one day, Joseph and the woman were alone in the house. Grabbing hold of his robe – Joseph's clothes are a repeated source of trouble to him, it seems – she again propositioned him. He fled from her presence, out of the house, leaving his garment in her hands. If Joseph was not naked when he fled, he must surely have been near-naked. [There was scarcely less urgency for Joseph, than there would later be for the young man in Mark's Gospel, who fled the scene of Jesus' arrest, also leaving his garment behind (Mk. 14:51–52).]

William Congreve's dictum, 'Hell has no fury, like a woman scorned', might have been coined with Potiphar's wife in mind. 'When she saw that he had left his garment in her hand' – as her husband had left all that belonged to him in Joseph's hands, verse 6 – 'and had fled outside, she called out to members of her household and said to them, "See, my husband has brought among us a Hebrew to insult us! He came in to me" (an obvious pun) "to lie with me, and I cried out with a loud voice; and when he heard me raise my voice and cry out, he left his garment beside me, and fled outside"' (verses 14–15).

Two things are striking about the woman's words. The first is the freedom with which she spoke disparagingly to the servants about her husband. She blames him for 'bringing a Hebrew among us'. It is quite possible that the servants were already resentful of Joseph's position in the household – an alien and a newcomer, achieving authority over them – and that Potiphar's wife was seeking to exploit that. But her words seem to be

exploiting not just any resentment among the servants towards
Joseph, but any towards Potiphar too. They are not the words of
a happily married woman.

Secondly, she calls Joseph, the slave, 'a Hebrew'. This is the
first occasion in the Bible that that association is made; but it will
become a repeated one in the Old Testament, especially in the
book of Exodus. The association is noteworthy, because the word
'Hebrew' is a relatively rare one in the Bible. Its use is concentrated in the opening two chapters of the book of Exodus, where
the enslavement of Israel is in focus (Ex. 1:15,16,19,22; 2:6,7,11,13).
It recurs in Exodus 21:3, Deuteronomy 15:12 and Jeremiah 34:9,
where the references are again to Hebrew slaves. The single
exception to this pattern is the earliest reference of all, in Genesis
14:13, where Abram is introduced as 'the Hebrew'; although even
there the point can be stretched: he is just about to receive word
that his nephew Lot has been captured. The association is all the
more startling, because the other repeated use of the word
'Hebrew' in the Old Testament is in relation to God: first of all in
Exodus (3:18; 5:11; 7:16; 9:1,13; 10:3) and ultimately also in the
book of Jonah (1:9), God is called 'the God of the Hebrews'.
Perhaps the relative rarity of the word in the Old Testament
reflects a pejorative association with slavery, which begins here in
the Joseph story (and compare Gen. 41:12). How like the God of
the Bible, then, that his name also becomes associated with a dis-
paraging term. What is God like? He is the kind of God who
makes himself a champion of slaves and the down-trodden, as
Joseph is in the process of discovering.

For at least the last 1500 years, the church in the west has been
a church in power. This has had many advantages but it has also
presented dangers. A church with many resources is not well
placed to trust wholly in the Lord. Conversely, a church in adversity is well placed to know the God of the Hebrews.

At present, the church in the west finds its status under threat.
Privileges and responsibilities it has taken for granted in the past
are now eroded. The future seems like an alien and forbidding
place. It is right for the church, moving into that future, to aspire for
growth and unity but meanwhile, there are lessons to learn. There
are benefits to be had for a church in adversity – and a renewal of
knowledge of 'the God of the Hebrews' is an obvious example.

In verses 17–18, Potiphar's wife repeats her charge to her husband almost word for word, as if the speech was now rehearsed – including the implication that he himself was responsible for this turn of events. She does, however, this time call Joseph 'a slave' – a word she had shrewdly not used previously, when making her appeal to his fellow slaves. Potiphar is enraged, and puts Joseph in prison – 'in the prison where the king's prisoners were kept'. As it happens, this is the prison over which Potiphar himself had responsibility, as 'the captain of the guard' (Gen. 39:1, cf. 40:3). Just as Judah had done with Tamar, Potiphar acts swiftly and severely and without any attempt to hear the defendant's side of the story. Joseph is incarcerated without any recourse to law, nor any hope of deliverance. Ironically, he is punished for doing right: 'His feet were hurt with fetters, his neck was put in a collar of iron' (Ps. 105:18). In material terms, his situation might have been better if he had succumbed to the overtures of Potiphar's wife. On the other hand, Potiphar knew what sort of man Joseph was and probably also what sort of woman his wife was. Perhaps the fact that Joseph suffered no worse fate than imprisonment reflects an inkling on Potiphar's part about the truth of what had happened. Later in the story (Gen. 40:3), it is clear that over time Potiphar's confidence in Joseph was restored sufficiently for him to entrust senior prisoners to his care (apparently by-passing the chief jailor). At least, it is fair to assume this is Potiphar. He is not named in Chapter 40: the reference is simply to 'the captain of the guard'; but this is how Potiphar is introduced in 39:1. The text at 40:3 also states that the prison in which Joseph found himself was 'in the house' of the captain of the guard: and in 41:12, Joseph is still described as 'a servant of the captain of the guard'. So perhaps his downfall wasn't so great after all – certainly, Potiphar kept him close by.

Scene Three: A Turn for the Better (The Lord is Present, verses 21–23)

21 But the LORD was with Joseph and showed him steadfast love; he gave him favour in the sight of the chief jailer. 22 The chief jailer committed to Joseph's care all the prisoners who were in the

prison, and whatever was done there, he was the one who did it. 23 The chief jailer paid no heed to anything that was in Joseph's care, because the LORD was with him; and whatever he did, the LORD made it prosper.

We are given no insight into Joseph's frame of mind in the immediate aftermath of his imprisonment. What resentment he may have felt towards either Potiphar or his wife, what struggles he may have had to retain his trust in God – the text is silent about these things.

The text moves on in verse 23 as follows: 'But the Lord was with Joseph'. When Scripture says, 'But the Lord' (as it does 76 times in the Old Testament), it is often good news. When Gideon, terrified, realises he has seen God face to face, we read: 'But the Lord said to him, "Peace, don't be afraid"' (Judg. 6:23). When the Psalmist ponders the afflictions of the righteous, he asserts, 'But the Lord rescues them from them all' (Ps. 34:19). When the apostle is deserted by all, he is still able to affirm, 'But the Lord stayed with me and gave me strength' (2 Tim. 4:17).

This is the wider context in which our text now continues, 'But the Lord was with Joseph and showed him steadfast love.' Even in Egypt, even in prison in Egypt, the Lord of covenant love was with Joseph. The result was that just as he had risen to a position of responsibility in Potiphar's house and knew success there, so in jail he rises to a position of responsibility and enjoys renewed success. Like Potiphar before him and Pharaoh after him, the chief jailor comes quickly to trust that he can leave matters in Joseph's hands: 'He paid no heed to anything that was in Joseph's care, because the Lord was with him.' The implication here may even be that, like Potiphar before him (verse 3) and Pharaoh after him (Gen. 41:39), the chief jailor also came to acknowledge Joseph's God.

Conclusion

Joseph's situation has gone from bad (a slave to Potiphar) to worse (an imprisoned slave to Potiphar), and the deterioration was all the more galling because of the success and prosperity he had known for some time in Potiphar's house. Yet this episode ends on a high note: success and prosperity return, albeit on a smaller scale, in a reduced sphere of influence. And although the text is silent, as we have noted, on Joseph's feelings about his predicament, the inference seems to be that, as he prospered, he was renewed in faith and trust in the Lord: he knew that the Lord was with him. Certainly there is no trace of the self-pity into which his father Jacob was plunged by the adversities that afflicted him (Gen. 37:34–35; 42:36–38). On the other hand, Joseph's prospects were bleak: a reasonably comfortable existence in the confines of the prison was as much as he could hope for.

Chapter Four

'Do not interpretations belong to God?'

(Genesis 40)

Introduction

At the end of the previous episode, it is understood that Joseph is in prison – the text does not specify for how long – and that he is prospering. But there are limits to his prosperity: he remains not just a slave, but an imprisoned one. In a hidden and painfully slow way, however, the purpose of God is still unfolding, as this next episode confirms. There may be no obvious improvement in Joseph's circumstances, but there is a significant development in his 'vocation' and training as 'the lord of the dream' (37:19) – one which will be of the utmost importance in the very next chapter: Joseph discovers that he is gifted not only in dreaming, but in discerning the meaning of dreams. Along the way, the reader discovers that Joseph's gift is not merely there for his own personal benefit – it becomes now the means by which the destinies of others are also revealed. His gifts are not just about the fulfilment of God's purpose in his own life, but in the lives of those around him – for good and ill.

Like the previous two chapters, this one can also be read in three parts: there are brief 'before' and 'after' sections, and a longer middle section in which the central action takes place. In scene one (verses 1–4), Joseph is joined in prison by two of Pharaoh's officers; in scene two (verses 5–19), both men relate to Joseph dreams that they have dreamed in the night; and in the final scene (verses 20–23), Joseph is left to languish in prison even though his dream interpretations are fulfilled. As in Chapter 37 and again in Chapter 41, two dreams are related side by side; but unlike on those other occasions, here the dreams are dreamt by two individuals and two separate, indeed opposite, interpretations apply.

Scene One: The Arrival of Pharaoh's Cupbearer and Baker (verses 1–4)

> 1 Some time after this, the cupbearer of the king of Egypt and his baker offended their lord the king of Egypt. 2 Pharaoh was angry with his two officers, the chief cupbearer and the chief baker, 3 and he put them in custody in the house of the captain of the guard, in the prison where Joseph was confined. 4 The captain of the guard charged Joseph with them, and he waited on them; and they continued for some time in custody.

What the cupbearer and the baker did to offend Pharaoh the text does not state. Whether they acted jointly or were only coincidentally imprisoned, again, we do not know. But in his anger, Pharaoh consigned both these officials to jail 'in the house of the captain of the guard' – Potiphar's house (see below, verse 7; and Gen. 37:36). And Potiphar entrusted them to Joseph, who 'waited on them'. For some time – again, the text does not specify the passage of time – these three were fellow-prisoners, with Joseph in a position of care over the other two.

Scene Two: The Dreams of Pharaoh's Cupbearer and Baker (verses 5–19)

> 5 One night they both dreamed – the cupbearer and the baker of the king of Egypt, who were confined in the prison – each his own dream, and each dream with its own meaning. 6 When Joseph came to them in the morning, he saw that they were troubled. 7 So he asked Pharaoh's officers, who were with him in custody in his master's house, 'Why are your faces downcast today?' 8 They said

to him, 'We have had dreams, and there is no one to interpret them.' And Joseph said to them, 'Do not interpretations belong to God? Please tell them to me.'

9 So the chief cupbearer told his dream to Joseph, and said to him, 'In my dream there was a vine before me, 10 and on the vine there were three branches. As soon as it budded, its blossoms came out and the clusters ripened into grapes. 11 Pharaoh's cup was in my hand; and I took the grapes and pressed them into Pharaoh's cup, and placed the cup in Pharaoh's hand.' 12 Then Joseph said to him, 'This is its interpretation: the three branches are three days; 13 within three days Pharaoh will lift up your head and restore you to your office; and you shall place Pharaoh's cup in his hand, just as you used to do when you were his cupbearer. 14 But remember me when it is well with you; please do me the kindness to make mention of me to Pharaoh, and so get me out of this place. 15 For in fact I was stolen out of the land of the Hebrews; and here also I have done nothing that they should have put me into the dungeon.'

16 When the chief baker saw that the interpretation was favourable, he said to Joseph, 'I also had a dream: there were three cake baskets on my head, 17 and in the uppermost basket there were all sorts of baked food for Pharaoh, but the birds were eating it out of the basket on my head.' 18 And Joseph answered, 'This is its interpretation: the three baskets are three days; 19 within three days Pharaoh will lift up your head – from you! – and hang you on a pole; and the birds will eat the flesh from you.'

After some time, the two men dreamt their parallel dreams. The following morning, Joseph came in and saw that they were troubled. It speaks volumes for the change in Joseph that he was sensitive to their mood. The self-absorbed teenager has given way to a self-aware adult, apparently more concerned with the predicaments of others than with his own. When he asks Pharaoh's officers, 'What's the matter?', there is no indication that he had any idea dreams were involved.

The men tell him that they have dreamt dreams 'and there is no-one to interpret them' (verse 8). In freedom, they would have known what to do. Had they dreamed portentous dreams outside the prison, they would have sought out those with a gift and reputation for dream interpretation: the wise men and magicians of Pharaoh's court (compare Gen. 41:8). But in prison, what are they to do?

Here Joseph makes his second 'confession of faith'. Having in the previous episode asked Potiphar's wife, 'How could I do such a wicked thing and sin against God', Joseph here asks a second question: 'Do not interpretations belong to God?' If Joseph was learning in Chapter 37 that the possession of the gifts of God carries no guarantee that they will be exercised in a godly way, he is about to discover further that it carries no guarantee as to the sphere in which they will be exercised. There is no guarantee that spiritual gifts will be exercised only in ever increasing spheres of influence and significance – but perhaps there is also some assurance here that with God no sphere is too small, too apparently inappropriate, for the flourishing of gifts he has given.

So Joseph invites the men to tell him their dreams, which they do one after the other. Clearly implicit is an assumption on Joseph's part that God will provide him with the interpretations. He may lack the arts of the Egyptian professionals; but he has faith and trust in God and some small firsthand experience of dreams and their meanings. Indeed, his assertion that the interpretation of dreams 'belongs to God' may be taken as an exclusive and therefore subversive assertion vis à vis the empire of Egypt. Whatever Pharaoh's power may be (and in the most obvious sense, Joseph is powerless in the face of it), there are limits to what he knows and what he can dictate, limits which Joseph senses may not, by the grace of God, apply to him. The future, in fact, belongs to God, not Pharaoh. The future is fixed by God, not Pharaoh. And Joseph presents himself as God's minister and agent.

Of course, the Egyptian courtiers have nothing to lose. So first the cupbearer speaks; and immediately, sure enough, Joseph is able to provide an interpretation. In only three days, the cupbearer's circumstances will change radically for the better: he will be released from prison and restored to his previous place in Pharaoh's court.

Having furnished the interpretation, however, Joseph goes on (verses 14–15): 'But remember me when it is well with you; please do me the kindness to make mention of me to Pharaoh, and so get me out of this place. For in fact I was stolen out of the land of the Hebrews; and here also I have done nothing that they should have put me into the dungeon' (literally, Joseph says, 'pit' – perhaps to make a link with the cistern in which he was thrown by his brothers). For all Joseph's growing maturity and faith, it is difficult to ignore the note of desperation that intrudes at this point. He sees in this sudden development an opportunity: if the cupbearer is about to go free, perhaps he is also. 'Get me out of this place!', he begs. And he rehearses the reason: not 'because I have helped to get you out', although return of favour is no doubt also implied, but 'because first, I was unjustly brought even to Egypt; and second, I was unjustly thrown into jail. I have done nothing to deserve this; I am doubly a victim.' He seems to lose sight of what he had earlier seemed to know so fully – that the future belongs to God, and that he himself has been entrusted with a mission from God. He is reduced to begging from the cupbearer what he might have been expected to seek from God. There is something unattractive about Joseph's attempt to give the providence of God a nudge here; although many of us are tempted to do so, when we see what appears to be an opening. It can be difficult to wait, and to wait, and to wait again for a better future; and to resist the temptation to press our claims inopportunely.

Encouraged by the outcome presented to his colleague, the baker relates his own dream (verses 16–17). It has such an obvious point of similarity, he inevitably hopes for a similar interpretation: where the cupbearer dreamt of three vine branches, the baker saw three cake baskets. But where the cupbearer had seen the fruition of his vine branches, enabling him to provide Pharaoh with a full cup of wine; the baker saw birds eating away at the baked food intended for Pharaoh. The difference is ominous and Joseph duly supplies the meaning: in three days, you will be hanged (or perhaps, 'decapitated').

The text doesn't appear to suggest that it was particularly distressing to Joseph to deliver this bad news; on the contrary, there is almost an element of mischief and gory delight in the way Joseph exploits the pun on the 'lifting up' of the two heads to convey his interpretation in verse 19 (The Gospel of John makes a similar pun in relation to Jesus' death in chapter 8:12; 12:32).

Joseph seems to be leading the baker on, to think that his fate will match the cupbearer's, only to deliver cruelly what you might call a sting in the tale.

Scene Three: The Departure of Pharaoh's Cupbearer and Baker (verses 20–23)

> 20 On the third day, which was Pharaoh's birthday, he made a feast for all his servants, and lifted up the head of the chief cupbearer and the head of the chief baker among his servants. 21 He restored the chief cupbearer to his cupbearing, and he placed the cup in Pharaoh's hand; 22 but the chief baker he hanged, just as Joseph had interpreted to them. 23 Yet the chief cupbearer did not remember Joseph, but forgot him.

Sure enough, three days later it was Pharaoh's birthday. Perhaps this was an anniversary well known to Joseph and the courtiers, though the text does not say so. Nor is it said how this anniversary prompted him to summon the cupbearer and baker; but he did so. He duly 'lifted up their heads': restoring the cupbearer to his previous post and hanging the baker.

One wonders how Joseph coped with the following few days and weeks. It is easy to imagine that the three days between his interpretation of the dreams and their fulfilment were laden with emotion: the cupbearer hoping earnestly that Joseph's interpretation might be proved true; the baker hoping equally earnestly that it might not; and Joseph, perhaps anxious to see whether or not his confession of faith in God was to be honoured.

And for Joseph, the days immediately following the departure of the two officials from prison were surely dizzy with excitement. He had, after all, explicitly urged the cupbearer to remember him. Over the next few days, he must have expected deliverance at any moment. At this point in the story, Joseph is twenty-eight years old (that is, thirty – as at 41:46 – less two years – as in 41:1). It is eleven years since he dreamt his own dreams. Even if he had not reflected on them much during that time, he must surely have done so now. He must have sensed in the fulfilment of these two latest dreams, the imminent fulfilment of his own. But as days stretched to weeks and months, his high hopes must have dwindled to fresh disappointment and heartache. So near and yet so far. For the episode ends by stating, with definite emphasis: 'yet the cupbearer did not remember Joseph, but forgot him' (verse 23). Forgotten by the cupbearer, Joseph is left to question whether he is remembered by God.

Prolonged adversity is bound to make the believer – and the believing community – ask that same question: Does God remember his people? The reader of the Joseph cycle is privy to an answer to which Joseph himself had no access. He may have felt forgotten, but the reader knows that he was not. As a result, the reader also has access to an encouragement, which Joseph was denied. The knowledge that there was a purpose in Joseph's continued imprisonment should give the church in adversity pause for thought. Might God not also have a purpose in its continued languishing? Joseph was not released before the right moment had come; and a church in adversity may not be either.

Chapter Five

'The Thing is Fixed by God'

(Genesis 41:1–40)

Introduction

When Chantelle won Channel 4's 'Celebrity Big Brother' in 2006, and was swept away in a whirl of money-spinning media opportunities, she was exhorted by her mother to 'live the dream'. When Alan Shearer retired from professional football and André Agassi from professional tennis (also both in 2006), they both said about their careers that they had 'lived the dream'. Ours is a culture that values the dream, but has narrow and exclusively positive expectations of it. 'The dream' is a fantasy of my heart's desire, the best that I could possibly ask or imagine; 'living the dream' is wish-fulfilment.

Dreams in Scripture are frequently more sobering. It is possible to find dreams in the Bible which are extremely positive: 'When the Lord restored the fortunes of Zion, we were like those who dream' (Ps. 126:1). But these are the exception, not the rule. On the whole, whether dreamt by the New Testament Joseph or the Magi in the opening chapters of Matthew's Gospel (1:20; 2:13), by Nebuchadnezer in Daniel (Chapters 2 and 4), by a Midianite soldier in the book of Judges (Judg. 7:13) or by the baker or Pharaoh in this Joseph cycle, dreams in Scripture tend to be troubling, disturbing, disquieting things – not at all the sort of thing any rational person would leap at the opportunity to 'live'.

Yet in the Joseph cycle, the sobering dreams as well as the heartening ones are for living: they are premonitions. Joseph began the cycle as the dreamer: it was his own future that he saw as he slept. He has become the interpreter of dreams: now it is the destinies of other people that he is required to spell out, although even in the case of the cupbearer and the baker, and certainly in Pharaoh's case in this episode in the story, his own destiny is also implicated.

But it is easy to exaggerate the significance of dreams in the Joseph cycle: although Joseph's own dreams dominate Chapter 37, the dreams of the cupbearer and baker dominate Chapter 40, and Pharaoh's dreams dominate Chapter 41, at this point the phenomenon reaches its climax and plays no further part in the story: there are no dreams in Chapters 42 – 50, in the last three-quarters of the cycle.

Genesis 41 has an unusual structure: it invites itself to be read in five sections of eight verses each. In the first eight verses, Pharaoh's dreams are introduced, but there is no one to interpret them. In the next scene, Joseph is summoned and his capacity as an interpreter of dreams is established. In verses 17 to 24, Pharaoh relates his dream to Joseph and bewails the failure of his magicians to explain them. In the penultimate scene, Joseph offers the interpretation; and in the final eight verses, Joseph moves on to offer advice on how Pharaoh should respond to his dreams – advice Pharaoh adopts without delay. There is a significant pattern to the invocation of God (or absence of it) through these five scenes.

Scene One: Pharaoh's Dreams (verses 1–8)

> 1 After two whole years, Pharaoh dreamed that he was standing by the Nile, 2 and there came up out of the Nile seven sleek and fat cows, and they grazed in the reed grass. 3 Then seven other cows, ugly and thin, came up out of the Nile after them, and stood by the other cows on the bank of the Nile. 4 The ugly and thin cows ate up the seven sleek and fat cows. And Pharaoh awoke. 5 Then he fell asleep and dreamed a second time; seven ears of grain, plump and good, were growing on one stalk. 6 Then seven ears, thin and blighted by the east wind, sprouted after them. 7 The thin ears swallowed up the seven plump and full ears. Pharaoh awoke, and it was a dream. 8 In the morning his spirit was troubled; so he sent

and called for all the magicians of Egypt and all its wise men.
Pharaoh told them his dreams, but there was no one who could
interpret them to Pharaoh.

It is two whole years before there is any change is Joseph's situation. He was almost certainly in prison for years, rather than
months, say, before his encounter with the cupbearer and had
evidently seen that encounter as offering a very real hope of his
deliverance. Presumably in the days immediately after the cupbearer's release, Joseph was in a state of high anticipation; presumably also, as days became weeks and weeks became months,
his hopes waned, and his daily expectation that he was about to
be freed soured. Here was further scope for Joseph to wallow in
self-pity and resentment; but the text offers no indication that he
did so.

In fact, Joseph is not 'on stage' in the first scene of this episode
in the story. In the first eight verses, there is no reference to Joseph
and also no reference to God. In terms of the shape of the passage, this turns out to be important. Instead, the spotlight falls on
Pharaoh.

Pharaoh is, of course, the epitome of power in Joseph's day.
His empire and his dynasty were legendary. But he is introduced
to us powerless: he is helpless in the face of his disturbing
dreams. He may be the focus of power in Egypt, used to issuing
messages; but here he is the passive one, receiving them. He is
used to being in control and getting what he wants; here he finds
his resources are inadequate. For once, Pharaoh is confronted
with his humanity: he is brought face to face with his limits. It can
be hard for an individual used to power to come to terms with a
new and unfamiliar powerlessness; and equally hard for an institution as powerful as the contemporary church in the west.

Pharaoh has dreamt, first, of two sets of cattle: he saw seven
'sleek and fat' cows, healthy and fit for slaughter, come up out of
the Nile and graze in the reedgrass beside the river – to this day,
cattle by the Nile seek respite in it from the sun. But the seven
sleek cows are followed by seven others, gaunt and ugly, which
proceed to eat them. Pharaoh then awoke, agitated by the dream.
But falling back to sleep he dreamt again – of two sets of ears of
grain: the first plump and good, the second thin and blighted;

and sure enough, the blighted ears swallow up the others. Again, Pharaoh wakes, agitated. By morning, his agitation has increased rather than diminished: 'his spirit was troubled' (literally, 'his spirit pounded', verse 8). So he sent for 'all the magicians of Egypt and all its wise men'. The comprehensive nature of the summons is emphasised: Egypt was famed in the Old Testament period for its wisdom and Pharaoh is leaving no stone unturned in his search for meaning. Everyone who can help him must help him. If help can be found in such a case, it can surely be found in Egypt. But no: 'Pharaoh told them his dreams, but there was no one who could interpret them to Pharaoh'.

Scene Two: Pharaoh Summons Joseph (verses 9–16)

> 9 Then the chief cupbearer said to Pharaoh, 'I remember my faults today. 10 Once Pharaoh was angry with his servants, and put me and the chief baker in custody in the house of the captain of the guard. 11 We dreamed on the same night, he and I, each having a dream with its own meaning. 12 A young Hebrew was there with us, a servant of the captain of the guard. When we told him, he interpreted our dreams to us, giving an interpretation to each according to his dream. 13 As he interpreted to us, so it turned out; I was restored to my office, and the baker was hanged.' 14 Then Pharaoh sent for Joseph, and he was hurriedly brought out of the dungeon. When he had shaved himself and changed his clothes, he came in before Pharaoh. 15 And Pharaoh said to Joseph, 'I have had a dream, and there is no one who can interpret it. I have heard it said of you that when you hear a dream you can interpret it.' 16 Joseph answered Pharaoh, 'It is not I; God will give Pharaoh a favourable answer.'

In the second scene of this episode, it is not only Joseph who is introduced onto the stage, but also God.

The emergency prompts the memory of the cupbearer, who in passing acknowledges his fault in forgetting Joseph. He recounts his experience to Pharaoh, even though to do so involves reminding him that he was once 'angry with his servants'. His testimony is all the more powerful for addressing two dreams: Joseph had been able to provide an accurate interpretation of each, involving a good outcome in one case and a poor one in the other. So at last Joseph is brought out of prison. Liberation comes quickly, when it finally comes. There is an urgency, a desperation about the moment that Joseph would not have envisaged, and an extraordinary need: he is summoned into the presence of Pharaoh. This requires new clothes and a shave (it was the Egyptian custom to shave the head).

After years in a dungeon, Joseph's horizons are suddenly extraordinarily wide. He is brought into the presence of the ruler of Egypt – and the presence, presumably, of a sheepish looking cupbearer. 'I have had a dream', Pharaoh says to him, 'and there is no one who can interpret it. I have heard it said of you that when you hear a dream, you can interpret it' (verse 15).

Joseph's response offers a further indication of the extent to which he has matured in the years of trial he has experienced. As a youth, modesty was not part of his skill set. He was conscious only of his own importance, his own destiny. He never made mention of God. Here, he is being flattered by the most powerful man in his world. 'I have heard it said of you that when you hear a dream, you can interpret it'. It is easy to imagine the seventeen year old Joseph replying, 'Yes, that's true'. But the thirty year old version answers, 'It is not I; God will give Pharaoh a favourable answer'. He deflects attention away from himself and his giftedness and onto God, the author of the gift. This is the third 'confession of faith' Joseph has made in the story; only this time, he frames a statement rather than a question. 'How can I do this great wickedness and sin against God?' (39:9) and 'Do not interpretations belong to God?' (40:8) give way to 'God will give Pharaoh a favourable answer' (41:16). For the first time, Joseph makes a claim on behalf of the God he serves. Given the circumstances, the claim was a considerable act of faith. He could not afford to be wrong.

Gifted and experienced as Joseph may be where dreams are concerned, he knows that what is being asked of him lies beyond his capacity to guarantee. He knows that like Pharaoh himself and like all the magicians and wise men of Egypt, he is a limited human being, utterly dependent on God. But he also knows that what is beyond human capacity is not beyond the capacity of

God and that what is impossible for human beings is possible with God. Such knowledge often escapes individuals who (or institutions which) have considerable resources of their own on which to rely. To know that what is impossible for human beings is possible with God is often the preserve of those who have exhausted their own capacity.

Scene Three: Pharaoh Relates his Dream to Joseph (verses 17–24)

> 17 Then Pharaoh said to Joseph, 'In my dream I was standing on the banks of the Nile; 18 and seven cows, fat and sleek, came up out of the Nile and fed in the reed grass. 19 Then seven other cows came up after them, poor, very ugly, and thin. Never had I seen such ugly ones in all the land of Egypt. 20 The thin and ugly cows ate up the first seven fat cows, 21 but when they had eaten them no one would have known that they had done so, for they were still as ugly as before. Then I awoke. 22 I fell asleep a second time and I saw in my dream seven ears of grain, full and good, growing on one stalk, 23 and seven ears, withered, thin, and blighted by the east wind, sprouting after them; 24 and the thin ears swallowed up the seven good ears. But when I told it to the magicians, there was no one who could explain it to me.'

In the third scene in this episode, Pharaoh relates his dreams. Verses 17–24 are a repetition therefore, almost word for word, of verses 1–8 – although there are some added touches. In relation to the first dream, Pharaoh reflects that the gaunt cows are not just 'ugly and thin' (verse 3), but 'poor, very ugly and thin' – the ugliest cows he had ever seen in Egypt (verse 19). And, more substantially, Pharaoh notes that when the thin and ugly cows had eaten up the sleek and fat ones, 'no one would have known that they had done so, for they were still as ugly as before'. That is almost the most frightening aspect of the nightmare: the ugly, thin cows stay ugly and thin even after consuming the sleek, fat ones. Their condition is not improved, even at that cost.

Similarly, in relation to the second dream, the second ears of grain are not just 'thin and blighted' (verse 6), but 'withered, thin and blighted' (verse 23). Pharaoh is not able to tame his dreams in the reliving of them: their capacity to trouble him is still growing.

As with the parallel scene one, there is no mention here of God.

Scene Four: Joseph Interprets the Dream for Pharaoh (verses 25–32)

> 25 Then Joseph said to Pharaoh, 'Pharaoh's dreams are one and the same; God has revealed to Pharaoh what he is about to do. 26 The seven good cows are seven years, and the seven good ears are seven years; the dreams are one. 27 The seven lean and ugly cows that came up after them are seven years, as are the seven empty ears blighted by the east wind. They are seven years of famine. 28 It is as I told Pharaoh; God has shown to Pharaoh what he is about to do. 29 There will come seven years of great plenty throughout all the land of Egypt. 30 After them there will arise seven years of famine, and all the plenty will be forgotten in the land of Egypt; the famine will consume the land. 31 The plenty will no longer be known in the land because of the famine that will follow, for it will be very grievous. 32 And the doubling of Pharaoh's dream means that the thing is fixed by God, and God will shortly bring it about.

In scene four (verses 25–32), Joseph is once more centre stage, and references to God proliferate. Indeed, Joseph makes a repeated and far greater claim on God's behalf: not only that he is able to interpret dreams, not even just that he knows the future and is able to disclose it, but that the future is subject to God's control.

Joseph goes straight to the point. Through his dreams, God is not just showing Pharaoh what is about to take place, but that what is about to take place is God's own doing. 'God has revealed to Pharaoh what he is about to do' (verse 25). And in case the point is missed: 'God has shown to Pharaoh what he is about to do' (verse 28).

The two dreams are one: seven years of plenty are coming for Egypt, to be followed by seven years of famine. The famine will be so severe that the years of plenty will be forgotten. 'And the doubling of Pharaoh's dream means that the thing is fixed by God, and God will shortly bring it about.' And the doubling of references to God at the end of the scene establishes Joseph's point: the future is not simply known to God, it is shaped and determined and 'fixed' by him. Not only so, but God is at work in the present: in Pharaoh, disturbing his sleep; in Egypt, preparing a nation for fat and for famine; and among his own people, including Joseph, to carry forward his good plan and purpose for them.

'Fixed by God' is an ambiguous phrase in a culture in which we speak of 'match fixing scandals' and 'fixes of drugs'. A cry of 'Fixed!' usually implies 'unfairly contrived'. 'Fixed' can also carry unfortunate connotations of rigidity as well as more helpful ones of mending. So what are we to make of it, when Joseph tells Pharaoh that the repetition of his dream means that 'the thing is fixed by God'? He certainly means that the future is in God's hands: it is directed by God. But this 'fixedness' does not lead Joseph into either complacency or resignation. On the contrary, it releases him to take responsibility for working with God to realise the future. A recovery of this kind of trust in a future 'fixed by God' is something that the church of God will need to nurture in the coming years.

Scene Five: Joseph Makes Policy for Pharaoh (verses 33–40)

> 33 Now therefore let Pharaoh select a man who is discerning and wise, and set him over the land of Egypt. 34 Let Pharaoh proceed to appoint overseers over the land, and take one-fifth of the produce of the land of Egypt during the seven plenteous years. 35 Let them gather all the food of these good years that are coming, and lay up grain under the authority of Pharaoh for food in the cities, and let them keep it. 36 That food shall be a reserve for the land against the seven years of famine that are to befall the land of Egypt, so that the land may not perish through the famine.' 37 The proposal pleased Pharaoh and all his servants. 38 Pharaoh said to his servants, 'Can we find anyone else like this – one in whom is the spirit of God?' 39 So Pharaoh said to Joseph, 'Since God has

shown you all this, there is no one so discerning and wise as you. 40 You shall be over my house, and all my people shall order themselves as you command; only with regard to the throne will I be greater than you.'

The transition between scene four and scene five at the end of verse 32 is not as obvious as at the end of each of the previous scenes, where a change of speaker marks it. Here, Joseph continues to speak. But the transition is real, nevertheless.

At this point, Joseph has completed the interpretation of the dreams. In terms of what he has been asked to provide by Pharaoh, his work is done. The reader might expect Pharaoh's response here. But Joseph continues, only in a new direction. He moves from the interpretation of the dreams to the recommendation of policy. 'That is what the dreams mean, Pharaoh', he is saying, 'and this is what you need to do about it'. As Calvin put it, 'true and lawful prophets of God do not barely predict what will happen in future; but propose remedies for impending evils.'

It might be thought that the revelation of the plan and purpose of God absolves human beings of responsibility for the future. Perhaps the faithful, blessed with a divine blueprint for what is to come, need only to sit back and watch: *'que sera, sera'*? In this case, however, the revelation of God prompts human planning rather than abolishing it. The proper response to the revelation of God's good will and purpose, for Joseph as well as for Pharaoh, is not resignation and the abrogation of responsibility, but faithful action.

With or without guile, Joseph effectively draws up a job description for himself. 'Let Pharaoh select a wise and discerning man and set him over Egypt' (verse 33) with overseers under him. Let them establish a system to ensure that reserves are built up during the years of plenty that are coming, 'so that the land may not perish through the famine' (verse 35).

The proposal pleases Pharaoh and his servants. The climax of this episode then follows. Pharaoh speaks of God. Previously, Pharaoh has been centre stage in scenes one and three, and Joseph centre stage in scenes two and four; and the only references to God have been on the lips of Joseph. But now Pharaoh speaks of God. First, he has a question for his servants: 'Can we find anyone else like this – one in whom is the spirit of God?' (Or, possibly, since the Hebrew word used here is *elohim*, 'the spirit of the gods'). And when his courtiers don't answer, and their silence is taken for their assent, Pharaoh then makes a statement to Joseph: 'Since God has [or 'the gods have'] shown you all of this, there is no one so discerning and wise as you'. Apparently, Pharaoh has accepted Joseph's interpretation at face value, and therefore accepted his recommendations too. He has not only believed what Joseph has said, he has chosen to act on it. He has accepted the words of Joseph as the Word of God. There is pre-sumably some risk here for Pharaoh: it will be fourteen years before Joseph's word is entirely fulfilled, and seven before there is any certain indication whether or not he has spoken the truth. Meanwhile, he has effectively placed the administration of his entire kingdom in the hands of a man he has only known for a few minutes, and a Hebrew slave at that.

The episode closes with Joseph's appointment as Pharaoh's right hand man. God enabled Joseph 'to win favour and to show wisdom when he stood before Pharaoh, king of Egypt, who appointed him ruler over Egypt and over all his household' (Acts 7:10).

Chapter Six

'God has made me forget, and be fruitful'

(Genesis 41:41–57)

Introduction

Personal names are important. They are important firstly to the people who bear them. Most people develop preferences for what they are called, choosing to be known (or definitely not known) by an abbreviation of their name, or substituting a middle name for a first name. But names are important also to the people who use them: they may be intensely private things, but they are also very public. Even, perhaps especially, in our global village, names are significant indicators of ethnic and social origins. They are often markers of the community not only from which a person has come, but to which a person belongs. For example, the entire Bulgarian soccer squad of about eighteen players is routinely composed only of people whose names end 'ov' or 'ev' – like Stanchev, Iliev and Hristov. However uncomfortable a fact it may be, this is why, in the current climate of terrorist threat, airport security organisations talk up the desirability of 'passenger profiling' on the basis, at least partly, of people's names. A 'Zadiq Mohammed' represents, on paper, a considerably greater potential threat than a 'Mary Jones'.

It goes without saying that in biblical times names were still more loaded with meaning than they are today – and especially with religious and spiritual meaning. And of all the books of the Bible in which this is true, it is nowhere more true than in

Genesis, where every birth is followed by a careful naming. A person's name came to be identified fully with its bearer and the bearer with the name, so that the speaking of a name was truly an invocation of the person. This was even true of God: his 'name' is something which has to be revealed, and which, when revealed, discloses his very self (see for example, Gen. 32:29).

That is the cultural context in which this next episode of the Joseph story has to be read. The episode falls into two parts and both parts are about names. There are grounds for reading the whole of Chapter 41 as a single episode, not of five eight-verse sections, but of seven eight-verse sections and a single one of nine-verses. On that reading, perhaps the penultimate section has the extra verse for emphasis: it is the moment Joseph is finally exalted to the position his dreams had indicated he would be. Here, however, these closing seventeen verses of chapter 41 are taken separately and in two 'scenes'. The first scene, in verses 41–49, is dominated by Egyptian names; the second, in verses 50–57, by Hebrew ones.

Scene One: Egyptian Names (verses 41–49)

41 And Pharaoh said to Joseph, 'See, I have set you over all the land of Egypt.' 42 Removing his signet ring from his hand, Pharaoh put it on Joseph's hand; he arrayed him in garments of fine linen, and put a gold chain around his neck. 43 He had him ride in the chariot of his second-in-command; and they cried out in front of him, 'Bow the knee!' Thus he set him over all the land of Egypt. 44 Moreover Pharaoh said to Joseph, 'I am Pharaoh, and without your consent no one shall lift up hand or foot in all the land of Egypt.' 45 Pharaoh gave Joseph the name Zaphenath-paneah; and he gave him Asenath daughter of Potiphera, priest of On as his wife. Thus Joseph gained authority over the land of Egypt. 46 Joseph was thirty years old when he entered the service of Pharaoh king of Egypt. And Joseph went out from the presence of Pharaoh, and went through all the land of Egypt. 47 During the seven plenteous years the earth produced abundantly. 48 He gathered up all the food of the seven years when there was plenty in the land of Egypt, and stored up food in the cities; he stored up in

every city the food from the fields around it. 49 So Joseph stored up grain in such abundance – like the sand of the sea – that he stopped measuring it; it was beyond measure.

In terms of the narrative, it is really only minutes since Joseph was languishing in a dungeon. Now he is appointed to a position of authority, not simply over all the prison or all of Potiphar's house, but over 'all of the land of Egypt'. What Potiphar or his wife made of this sudden reversal of fortune, we can only guess. Indeed, what Joseph made of it is not clear either: he makes no verbal response to Pharaoh's decision.

As Pharaoh makes the appointment, Christian readers will be reminded of the welcome that greeted the Prodigal Son: like him, Joseph is given a ring on his finger and garments of fine linen. If the coat he was given by his father Jacob was splendid, it was nothing to the robes in which he is now clothed by Pharaoh. And when he is invited to ride in the chariot of Pharaoh's second in command, and the people are exhorted to 'Bow the knee!' (verse 43), Joseph must surely have remembered those early dreams. It may have been far from apparent to him, how his family might one day be among those bowing to him; but that prospect must have seemed significantly closer from the chariot than it seemed from the prison cell.

Pharaoh retains his own ultimate authority – but everything else he gives to Joseph, including a new Egyptian name and an Egyptian wife (verse 45). This represents a moment of great potential danger for the newly liberated slave. How easy it might have been for a man who had suffered such deprivation for so long to rationalise the opportunity for self-indulgence. How easy for Joseph to abuse his freedom and authority on the grounds that he had suffered unjustly for long enough: he deserved some compensation, surely? How easy, in fact, for Joseph to turn his back on his Hebrew roots, his family and his faith. It can, of course, be easier to forget God in times of prosperity than in times of adversity. How easy for Joseph to become 'Zaphenath-paneah' (verse 45), not just in Pharaoh's eyes, but in his own. How easy to throw himself, not just into Egypt's crisis, but into Egypt's culture and language and religious traditions. How easy for Joseph to abandon the family of Jacob for the family of Potiphera, priest of On (verse 45).

But Joseph does not linger in Pharaoh's presence. The thirty year old Joseph doesn't dwell in nostalgia on his seventeen years of freedom in Canaan, or in regret on his thirteen years of captivity in Egypt. He departs instead on a nation-wide tour, looking to the future. He sets to work. The following seven years are a time of plenty not just for himself, but for the whole land. 'During the seven plenteous years the earth produced abundantly' (verse 47). So Joseph gathered up the excess and stored it up in the cities; there was so much of it ('such abundance, like the sand of the sea', verse 49), that he stopped keeping count of it.

Scene Two: Hebrew Names (verses 50–57)

> 50 Before the years of famine came, Joseph had two sons, whom Asenath daughter of Potiphera, priest of On, bore to him. 51 Joseph named the firstborn Manasseh, 'For,' he said, 'God has made me forget all my hardship and all my father's house.' 52 The second he named Ephraim, 'For God has made me fruitful in the land of my misfortunes.' 53 The seven years of plenty that prevailed in the land of Egypt came to an end; 54 and the seven years of famine began to come, just as Joseph had said. There was famine in every country, but throughout the land of Egypt there was bread. 55 When all the land of Egypt was famished, the people cried to Pharaoh for bread. Pharaoh said to all the Egyptians, 'Go to Joseph; what he says to you, do.' 56 And since the famine had spread over all the land, Joseph opened all the storehouses, and sold to the Egyptians, for the famine was severe in the land of Egypt. 57 Moreover, all the world came to Joseph in Egypt to buy grain, because the famine became severe throughout the world.

Before the years of famine came, Joseph experienced further blessing. Two sons were born to him; and it is a mark of Joseph's determination to resist the temptations he was facing to embrace life as an Egyptian, that he gave his sons Hebrew names. The first he calls 'Manasseh' (literally, 'Making to forget'), 'For,' he said, 'God has made me forget all my hardship and all my father's house' (verse 51). The emphasis is on the first half of the clause and the reference to 'his father's house' might best be understood as follows: 'God has made me forget all my hardship and has dulled the grief of being torn from my father's house.' The second he named 'Ephraim' (literally something like, 'To be fruit-ful'), 'For God has made me fruitful in the land of my misfor-tunes'. These are not just Hebrew names, in other words; they are names of faith, names which refer to God. They reflect Joseph's own faith and trust in the God of his fathers, and his intention to bring up his children in that faith. In so far as he is able to do it, Joseph is acting to secure the future of his part in the Lord's fam-ily.

The names Joseph chooses for his sons both refer to God – both Joseph and his sons derive their identity precisely from that rela-tionship; but both also refer to Joseph's history and experience. Our postmodern culture is notoriously reluctant to accept that our identity is derived from our history. We prefer to think we can reinvent ourselves indefinitely. Every time I sign on in an internet chat-room, I can be a new 'me'. But the reality is that my identity is formed, in part, by the story of my life so far and that of my community. This is as true for an institution like a congre-gation or a denomination as it is for an individual. For Joseph, as for every person, two parts of his history are especially signifi-cant: relationships and place – his family ('his father's house' in verse 51) and the promised land (implicit perhaps when Joseph speaks, in relation to the name 'Ephraim' of 'the land of my mis-fortunes' in verse 52: the name recalls that Egypt is not his home-land and implies that there is another land, which is not a place of misfortune but of blessing). When Joseph says 'God has made me fruitful', he is not simply referring to the success and pros-perity he has enjoyed in Egypt: he is laying hold of God's prom-ise to his fathers, of people and land.

When the seven years of plenty come to an end, the famine begins, just as Joseph had said it would. To emphasise the sever-ity of the famine, the text next contains a 'chiasmus'. A chiasmus is a common device in Hebrew literature, in which a text has a symmetrical shape: ABC in the first half of a text is followed by its reflection, CBA, in the second half. In this example, a reference to the famine 'in every country' at the end of verse 54 is followed in verse 55 by references first to the famine in Egypt and then to the role played by Joseph. In verses 56–57, the sequence is reversed: references to Joseph and the situation in Egypt in verse 56 are followed in verse 57 as the passage ends, by a reference to the famine 'throughout the world'. It can depicted as follows:

A *(v 54): every country*
B *(v 55): the land of Egypt*
C *(v 55): Joseph*

C *(v 56): Joseph*
B *(v 56): the land of Egypt*
A *(v 57): throughout the world*

All three elements in the chiasmus are important. First, the narrative alerts us to the fact that the famine is not confined to Egypt: there was a dearth of food in every land, 'but in Egypt there was bread' – so it will come as no surprise when the brothers arrive in search of food. Secondly, the text makes clear that the famine was also severe in Egypt, so that action was needed. But thirdly and most emphatically, it is Joseph whose action brings the people the help they need. When the people cry out to Pharaoh, his response is to say: 'Go to Joseph – and do whatever he tells you'. Christian readers will recall Mary saying similar words about Jesus in John 2:5. It is Joseph who opens the storehouses, Joseph who sells the grain both to the Egyptians and to 'all the world'.

Chapter Seven

'What is this God has done?'

(Genesis 42)

Introduction

On the whole, we are quicker to discern the hand of God at work when things go well than when things go badly. In a sense this is thoroughly appropriate. If God is as he is revealed in Jesus, then it is appropriate to expect him to act in loving and merciful ways. It is appropriate to expect that he will bless those he has created in his own image and seek their benefit and fulfilment. But it does not follow that when bad things happen, it is necessarily outside the good will and purpose of God for us. This is one of the enduring lessons in the book of Joseph. Ultimately, 'all is well': Joseph ends the story wealthy and wise and re-united with his father and brothers. But even at that point, let alone part way through the drama, it may be foolish to assume that he and Jacob and his brothers were quick to find the journey 'worth it'. Forgiveness and reconciliation do not come cheaply, as this episode in the story begins to illustrate. A complete restoration of trust between Joseph and his brothers was only slowly and painfully attained. This is part of the message of the remaining chapters of the story.

In episode seven, the focus of the story shifts. There is a coherence in Chapters 39 to 41 themselves – a story within the story: they chart Joseph's rise to leadership in Egypt. There is a similar coherence in Chapters 42 to 45: they chart his rise, it might be said, to leadership in his own family. Throughout Chapters 39 to 41, the action has taken place in Egypt. In Chapter 41, a definite climax is achieved and the focus now shifts, if only temporarily, to Canaan. The next such climax will come in Chapter 45, when Jacob and Joseph are reunited.

Episode seven of the Joseph cycle has three scenes. In the first (verses 1 to 5) Jacob and his sons are together in Canaan; in the second (verses 6 to 29) Joseph and his brothers are together in Egypt; and in the last (verses 29 to 38) Jacob is again with his sons in Canaan.

Scene One: Jacob and Sons in Canaan (verses 1–5)

> 1 When Jacob learned that there was grain in Egypt, he said to his sons, 'Why do you keep looking at one another? 2 I have heard,' he said, 'that there is grain in Egypt; go down and buy grain for us there, that we may live and not die.' 3 So ten of Joseph's brothers went down to buy grain in Egypt. 4 But Jacob did not send Joseph's brother Benjamin with his brothers, for he feared that harm might come to him. 5 Thus the sons of Israel were among the other people who came to buy grain, for the famine had reached the land of Canaan.

In the first verse of Chapter 42, the change of scene is abrupt. There is a hint in the closing words of Chapter 40 ('the famine became severe throughout the world'); but it is nevertheless a swift transition from Egypt back to Canaan, and from Joseph back to Jacob, the last reference to whom was in the penultimate verse of Chapter 37. But the change of scene is readily explained: the famine has reached Canaan (verse 3).

The change of scene is not, however, echoed by any change in Jacob. The Jacob we encounter at the start of Chapter 42 is very much the same person last seen in Chapter 37:35, bewailing his lost son and refusing to be comforted. At the start of Chapter 42 he is still trapped in his grief despite the passage of twenty years. It is not that after twenty years Jacob might be expected to have 'got over it': grief is not ever truly 'got over'. But nor would we expect Jacob to be stuck in his grief. Even where the sudden loss of a child is concerned, there is a natural movement and progression in our grief, which enables us increasingly to re-establish and attend to relationships with others, for example, or the ordinary demands of life and work. And there is something self-indulgent about the occasions when a person shows no such movement or development over a period of two decades. Thus when Jacob speaks, the note of peevish self-pity is still in his voice: 'Why do you just look at one another?', he complains to his sons, 'Go down to Egypt and get the food we need, so that we may live and not die'.

In one other respect, too, Jacob has not changed. When the brothers go, Jacob refuses to send Benjamin (the youngest son and the only other son, besides Joseph, born to his favourite wife, Rachel). Joseph may be lost, but Jacob has found a new favourite, another 'son of his old age' (compare Gen. 37:3).

So ten of Joseph's brothers (rather than 'ten of Jacob's sons' interestingly, in verse 3) join the many others going in search of food in Egypt.

Scene Two: Joseph and Brothers in Egypt (verses 6–28)

6 Now Joseph was governor over the land; it was he who sold to all the people of the land. And Joseph's brothers came and bowed themselves before him with their faces to the ground. 7 When Joseph saw his brothers, he recognised them, but he treated them like strangers and spoke harshly to them. 'Where do you come from?' he said. They said, 'From the land of Canaan, to buy food.' 8 Although Joseph had recognised his brothers, they did not recognise him. 9 Joseph also remembered the dreams that he had dreamed about them. He said to them, 'You are spies; you have come to see the nakedness of the land!' 10 They said to him, 'No, my lord; your servants have come to buy food. 11 We are all sons of one man; we are honest men; your servants have never been spies.' 12 But he said to them, 'No, you have come to see the nakedness of the land!' 13 They said, 'We, your servants, are twelve brothers, the sons of a certain man in the land of Canaan; the youngest, however, is now with our father, and one is no more.' 14 But Joseph said to them, 'It is just as I have said to you; you are spies! 15 Here is how you shall be tested: as Pharaoh lives, you shall not leave this place unless your youngest brother comes here!

16 Let one of you go and bring your brother, while the rest of you remain in prison, in order that your words may be tested, whether there is truth in you; or else, as Pharaoh lives, surely you are spies.' 17 And he put them all together in prison for three days. 18 On the third day Joseph said to them, 'Do this and you will live, for I fear God: 19 if you are honest men, let one of your brothers stay here where you are imprisoned. The rest of you shall go and carry grain for the famine of your households, 20 and bring your youngest brother to me. Thus your words will be verified, and you shall not die.' And they agreed to do so. 21 They said to one another, 'Alas, we are paying the penalty for what we did to our brother; we saw his anguish when he pleaded with us, but we would not listen. That is why this anguish has come upon us.' 22 Then Reuben answered them, 'Did I not tell you not to wrong the boy? But you would not listen. So now there comes a reckoning for his blood.' 23 They did not know that Joseph understood them, since he spoke with them through an interpreter. 24 He turned away from them and wept; then he returned and spoke to them. And he picked out Simeon and had him bound before their eyes. 25 Joseph then gave orders to fill their bags with grain, to return every man's money to his sack, and to give them provisions for their journey. This was done for them. 26 They loaded their donkeys with their grain, and departed. 27 When one of them opened his sack to give his donkey fodder at the lodging place, he saw his money at the top of the sack. 28 He said to his brothers, 'My money has been put back; here it is in my sack!' At this they lost heart and turned trembling to one another, saying, 'What is this that God has done to us?'

Genesis 42 verse 6 might have been expected to be a climax of the Joseph story. The story passes over the question of how these particular visitors to Egypt in search of food find themselves in the presence of the governor of the land; but the fact is that after twenty years apart, Joseph and his brothers are together again. Neither Joseph nor the brothers were expecting a reunion, of course; and the brothers are not even aware that it is taking place. Unlike Jacob, confronted with Joseph's coat in Chapter 37, and Judah, confronted by his personal effects in Chapter 38, the brothers do not recognise what is in front of them: they do not see their brother, only 'the governor of the land' (verse 6). Why should they recognise him? It has been many years since they saw him; he is out of context, probably still clean-shaven, dressed in the robes of an Egyptian aristocrat and speaking a language they do not understand. And in partial fulfilment of Joseph's first dream, 'they bow themselves before him with their faces to the ground' (verse 6). It is only a partial fulfilment, even of the first dream, because Benjamin is not with them.

But Joseph recognises his brothers: although they too may have changed, they are 'in context', in the sense that they are a band of brothers from the land of Canaan who are not presenting themselves otherwise, dressed and speaking in the way Joseph would have expected them to dress and speak (the issue of 'recognition' is emphasised in verse 8). And it is hard to escape the feeling that the story might have unfolded differently from this moment onwards. As it is, Joseph chooses 'to treat them like strangers and speak harshly to them' (verse 7). It is not clear that this was a desirable or necessary path for Joseph to take. Commentators are often at pains to excuse Joseph here, and to suggest that it was necessary for him to 'test' his brothers, to establish whether or not they had changed. But it is seldom explained why such a test might be necessary (would he never have disclosed himself to them if they had failed the test?), or whether 'the test' could not have been conducted in any other way. Even if, 'remembering his dreams' (verse 9), Joseph is setting out to establish the extent of his brothers' growth and repentance, it is not obvious that this is his role. Does that responsibility not lie with God? In other words, if Joseph did not respond at once with delight, generosity and for-giveness to the presence of his brothers, it may well owe more to an understandable resurgence of unresolved anger and a desire for some kind of revenge, than to a divinely prompted intention to assess and assist his brothers' spiritual development. Perhaps at a distance from them, Joseph had achieved some kind of peace with his brothers for what they had done; but suddenly face to face with them it is a different matter. 'Remembering his dreams' (verse 9) also meant remembering how and why his brothers acted in the way that they did. The upshot is that Joseph still has work to do before he can be reconciled to the brothers who betrayed him. Meanwhile, the path he chooses to take will bring considerable distress on his brothers and his father.

So his initial and instinctive (rather than calculated) response is to accuse them of being spies. When his brothers deny it (verses 10–11) and give him a brief and truthful summary of their situation, Joseph presses the accusation and prompts them to give a fuller account. Their words bear close reading. 'We are', they say, 'twelve brothers'. They still count Joseph among their number. 'The youngest', they go on, 'is now with our father, and one is no more.' Here, in his presence, the ten are put in mind of the brother they have eliminated from the family. They do not say he is 'dead'. That has been the pretence at home for twenty years, and they might have been expected to maintain the fiction out of habit; but they sense that the truth is required, and they resort to a euphemism: 'one is no more'. This is not a full and frank account – they signally fail to take any responsibility – but it is a step towards reality.

For the third time, Joseph accuses them of being spies. He then sets the terms of a test: one of his brothers is to return home to get Benjamin; the others will remain in prison. As far as the brothers are concerned then, the test is 'Are you "honest men" or are you spies?'; but Joseph and they already know full well they are not spies. As far as Joseph is concerned, the test is 'Are you "honest men" and have you changed? Or are you the dishonest men who sold me into slavery (and – though Joseph is not privy to this part of the story – lied to your father about it)? Indeed: is Benjamin, my full brother, really still alive, or have you done away with him as well?' As far as the reader is concerned, however, Joseph also faces a test. Has he changed enough to be able to forgive them from his heart and is he prepared for how costly that will prove?

While they ponder the test, Joseph puts them in prison for three days (verse 17). In all probability, we are to envisage that the brothers are now in the very prison in which Joseph spent so long. Where they once flung him into a pit, Joseph has now turned the tables on them. Three days is a long time in prison, when the future is unknown; but after three days, the brothers are brought before Joseph again. It seems that Joseph himself has been experiencing twinges of conscience. He is not ready to reprieve his brothers altogether, but he does mitigate the terms of the 'test'. 'Do I not fear God?', he says to them. He may as yet not be fully aware how far his fear of God will press him to go towards reconciliation with his brothers, but he has begun to sense the direction in which it presses him. Instead of releasing one brother and keeping the remaining nine in prison, Joseph is now proposing to release nine and to imprison only the remaining one. In any case, the earlier plan had a flaw: if only one brother had been released to return home, how on earth would he have managed to take with him even a fraction of the grain required to ensure the life of the whole of Jacob's family in the year ahead?

The brothers agree, but sorrowfully. They are contrite: 'Alas', they say (verse 21), 'we are paying the penalty for what we did to our brother . . . That is why this anguish has come upon us.' This is the first sign of their penitence; a second will follow at the end of the chapter. It emerges also, what was not reported in Chapter 37, that Joseph had pleaded in anguish with them at the time, not to do with him as they planned. Reuben, who sought (if half–heartedly) to intervene to save Joseph cannot resist an oldest brother's 'I told you so': 'Did I not tell you not to wrong the boy?' He can't bring himself to name Joseph, and evidently still thinks of him as the teenager he was. 'You would not listen to me, and now we are paying for his blood'.

Joseph eavesdrops on this dialogue. The brothers have no reason to believe he can understand them: he has been speaking to them with an interpreter. And when he hears their contrition and mutual recriminations, he weeps. He has to leave the room to compose himself. Again, the reader is left wondering why, at this point, Joseph does not come clean and make himself known to his brothers. Surely they have now passed the only test that matters to Joseph: the evidence is there, before *his* eyes that they regret what they did to him and have changed. But he persists in his plan: he picks out Simeon and has him bound before *their* eyes. Why Simeon is picked out it not clear. Perhaps Reuben is spared because he is the nearest thing Joseph has to an ally among the ten, and Simeon is chosen because he is the next oldest. Whatever the reason, Simeon is led away in chains and the brothers are forced to watch him go, just as they had previously watched Joseph led away. The remaining brothers are then faced with repeating a piece of their own history – it falls to them a second time to return home and explain the loss of one of their number.

Joseph, meanwhile, has not stopped his manipulations and interferences. He gives orders for the brothers' bags to be filled with grain, and for their money to be returned to their sacks and for provisions for the journey home to be provided for them. So the brothers load their donkeys and depart.

At the place of lodging (presumably a day's journey later), one of the brothers opens a sack and finds his money returned. When he cries out to his brothers to let them know what he has found, they lose heart and turn trembling to each other: 'What is this that God has done to us?' they ask. Joseph of course is not privy to this last exclamation; but the reader knows that like him, the brothers also fear God and have come to see his hand at work in their lives. In respect of the money, their consciences are clear; but in respect of their brother, they aren't. Perhaps the thought of the twenty pieces of silver they once gained (Gen 37:28) by selling him into slavery has returned to haunt them. In fact, it was Joseph and his staff who replaced the money in the brother's sack; but, not for the last time in this story, divine and human actions are in concert.

Scene Three: Jacob and Sons in Canaan (verses 29–38)

29 When they came to their father Jacob in the land of Canaan, they told him all that had happened to them, saying, 30 'The man, the lord of the land, spoke harshly to us, and charged us with spying on the land. 31 But we said to him, "We are honest men, we are not spies. 32 We are twelve brothers, sons of our father; one is no more, and the youngest is now with our father in the land of Canaan." 33 Then the man, the lord of the land, said to us, "By this I shall know that you are honest men: leave one of your brothers with me, take grain for the famine of your households, and go your way. 34 Bring your youngest brother to me, and I shall know that you are not spies but honest men. Then I will release your brother to you, and you may trade in the land."' 35 As they were emptying their sacks, there in each one's sack was his bag of money. When they and their father saw their bundles of money, they were dismayed. 36 And their father Jacob said to them, 'I am the one you have bereaved of children: Joseph is no more, and

Simeon is no more and now you would take Benjamin. All this has happened to me!' 37 Then Reuben said to his father, 'You may kill my two sons if I do not bring him back to you. Put him in my hands, and I will bring him back to you.' 38 But he said, 'My son shall not go down with you, for his brother is dead, and he alone is left. If harm should come to him on the journey that you are to make, you would bring down my grey hairs with sorrow to Sheol.'

The final scene in this episode has a simple structure: in verses 29 to 34, the brothers, on arrival home, tell their father what has happened and why Simeon has not returned with them; then, in verse 35, the other brothers open their sacks and find their money returned; and finally, in verses 36 to 38, Jacob responds to both these two developments.

In the first part (verses 29–34), there is an obvious irony in hearing the brothers repeat to the father to whom they have lied about the single most important event in his life for over twenty years, that they are 'honest men' (verses 31,33,34); and in hearing Joseph, about whom this lie has been told, referred to as 'the man, the lord of the land'. The account they offer their father is an abbreviation, but mostly word for word, of verses 9 to 20 – with the exception of the euphemistic allusion to Joseph in verse 13, which is subtly omitted, and the reference to their father, included here out of respect for Jacob and omitted earlier.

In verse 35, there is some sort of reprise of verse 28: the remaining nine brothers open their sacks (which oddly have not been opened on the journey before now) to find their money has been returned to them. Once again, this apparent good news causes dismay not rejoicing. On the face of it, the brothers have returned home with not only the grain their family so desperately needs, but the money they had spent to procure it. It's the equivalent of a modest win on the National Lottery, but it seems an ominous sign even to Jacob.

In the closing verses, we are given a further insight into Jacob's state of mind and heart. We look in vain for some mark of the man who dreamt of, and knew the blessing of God at Bethel ('I am with you and will keep you wherever you go . . . I will not leave you until I have done what I promised you', Gen 28:15), and who 'strove with God and with his fellow human beings' at the Jabbok river 'and prevailed' (Gen. 32:28). Rather, Jacob is presented as a pessimistic and mean man. 'I am the one you have bereaved of children' he says – at least insinuating, if not asserting outright, that his sons are responsible for his loss of Joseph as well as Simeon; and giving up at once all hope of seeing Simeon again. 'All this has happened to me!' A more self-pitying exclamation it would be hard to frame. There is no thought for Simeon's own life, say, or for his wife and children, whose husband and father has failed to return with the rest.

Reuben attempts to rally his father, offering his own sons as surety that he will deliver Benjamin safely home if Jacob will allow them to return to Egypt with him, to secure Simeon's release. But Jacob has no desire to risk anything with Benjamin: 'My son shall not go down with you', he says, 'for his brother is dead and he alone is left.' How that sounded in the ears of the other nine surviving sons of their father, the text does not say. 'If harm should come to Benjamin on the journey you propose to make, you would bring down my gray hairs in sorrow to Sheol.' Simeon, it seems, can be written off. Jacob is already determined to 'go down in sorrow to Sheol': that ironically became his 'reason for living', twenty years before (37:35). But to lose Benjamin would hasten the day of that descent. A sadder, smaller vision of life is hard to imagine. There is no faith, no hope in Jacob; only despair.

Chapter Eight

'God grant you mercy and be gracious to you!'

(Genesis 43)

Introduction

There is a common misunderstanding in the church, that the character of God in the Old Testament is different from the character of God in the New: that the Old Testament God is angry and severe, where the New Testament God is full of love and mercy; that the Old Testament shows us the frown on God's face and the New Testament his smile. The implication (or even explanation) is sometimes that the covenant between God and his people has a different basis in the Old Testament and in the New. In the Old Testament, it is sometimes said, a relationship with God is based on human effort, on the keeping of covenant law, whereas in the New, the relationship is based on divine grace.

This is a misunderstanding, and a serious one. God has only one 'face', one nature, one character. The very real differences between the Old Testament and the New, are differences of degree only, not of kind: the face of God comes into sharper focus in the New Testament, and most sharply of all in the gospel accounts of the life of Jesus.

If the Old Testament testifies to the anger and severity of God, so does the New. And if the New Testament emphasises the grace and mercy of God – so does the Old. Because the nature and character of God is one, there has only ever been one basis of his relationship with human beings: the covenant of grace. The law of what Christians call 'the Old Covenant' was a gift of grace: God had already chosen his people in Abraham and redeemed them from slavery through Moses by his grace, before he gave them, as a gift, the law. Conversely, under the New Covenant, election and redemption are by grace; but there is also the gracious summons to a life of holiness in response. It should surprise no one, therefore, that one of the most commonly repeated verses in the whole of the Old Testament says this: 'The Lord is gracious and merciful, slow to anger and abounding in steadfast love.'

Indeed, there are indications that this verse has a programmatic quality for the Old Testament. For one thing, it occurs first in Exodus 34:6, in a passage in which the Lord reveals his essence (his name) to Moses. For another, it comes in each of the three major divisions of the Hebrew Scriptures: the Law (in Ex. 34:6), the Prophets (in Joel 2:13 and Jon. 4:2); and the writings (in Ps. 86:5; 103:8; 145:8 and Neh. 9:17). And thirdly, though it's not always clear how much weight to place on such a thing, the phrase comes seven times in all – which is, in Scripture, the number of wholeness and completion.

And then, of course, it is necessary to look beyond the simple occurrences of the text, to the passages in the Old Testament which illustrate it – of which Genesis 43 is a good example. The grace and mercy of God lie just beneath the surface of this chapter. It falls into two parts, as a drama in two acts. The first act in the drama is in verses 1–14: it is set in Canaan, and the cast consists of Jacob and his ten sons. The second act is in verses 15–34: it is set in Egypt and the cast consists of Joseph and his eleven brothers (and a steward). The first act has only a single scene; the second act has multiple scenes. The key word in act one is 'mercy'; and in act two, it is 'grace'.

Act 1 (verses 1–14, set in Canaan): A God of Mercy

1 Now the famine was severe in the land. 2 And when they had eaten up the grain that they had brought from Egypt, their father said to them, 'Go again, buy us a little more food.' 3 But Judah said to him, 'The man solemnly warned us, saying, "You shall not see my face unless your brother is with you." 4 If you will send our

brother with us, we will go down and buy you food; 5 but if you will not send him, we will not go down, for the man said to us, "You shall not see my face, unless your brother is with you."' 6 Israel said, 'Why did you treat me so badly as to tell the man that you had another brother?' 7 They replied, 'The man questioned us carefully about ourselves and our kindred, saying, "Is your father still alive? Have you another brother?" What we told him was in answer to these questions. Could we in any way know that he would say, "Bring your brother down"?' 8 Then Judah said to his father Israel, 'Send the boy with me, and let us be on our way, so that we may live and not die – you and we and also our little ones. 9 I myself will be surety for him; you can hold me accountable for him. If I do not bring him back to you and set him before you, then let me bear the blame forever. 10 If we had not delayed, we would now have returned twice.' 11 Then their father Israel said to them, 'If it must be so, then do this: take some of the choice fruits of the land in your bags, and carry them down as a present to the man – a little balm and a little honey, gum, resin, pistachio nuts, and almonds. 12 Take double the money with you. Carry back with you the money that was returned in the top of your sacks; perhaps it was an oversight. 13 Take your brother also, and be on your way again to the man; 14 may God Almighty grant you mercy before the man, so that he may send back your other brother and Benjamin. As for me, if I am bereaved of my children, I am bereaved.'

The opening words of Chapter 43 imply a passage of time. It is weeks or months – though to judge from verse 10 probably not years – since the events of Chapter 42. One of the intriguing features of the Joseph story is how little it dwells on the experience of Simeon in captivity: we don't know how much contact he may have had with Joseph in that time, or what the conditions were in which he was held. Presumably, he was still in the very prison in which Joseph himself had spent so long. And presumably, he was counting the days until his release. At first, he will have been mentally following their brothers' journey home, and imagining the story they will have had to tell their father on arrival. After that, with mounting frustration, he will have been calculating how long it might take them to return with Benjamin to secure his release. And finally, in some desperation, he will have been forced to conclude that something had gone wrong. But the reader is given no insight into Simeon's experience, just as he is apparently given no insight into what was actually happening at home. The reader knows, from the way Chapter 42 ends, that Jacob was implacably opposed to the only course of action that would secure Simeon's early release. But Simeon does not know this; nor indeed does Joseph. Their response is hidden by the text, which focuses entirely for this part of the story on events in Canaan. And as we observe the interaction between Jacob and his brothers, we are invited to ponder the ways of God. As we assess the characters of the father and his sons, we are invited to do so against the character of God.

At the close of Chapter 42, Jacob is fearful; his sons, courageous. Reuben knows not only what it is right to do (risk his own life and happiness in the attempt to deliver Simeon); but also what is expedient to do (maintain the trust of the governor of Egypt, to whom they will likely need to return for more food). But Jacob can see no further than his own past losses and potential future loss.

In Chapter 43, it is Judah who picks up where Reuben had left off. The famine in Canaan is severe and the grain from Egypt is exhausted. When Jacob suggests a return visit, it is Judah who confronts him with reality. There is no prospect of a fruitful expedition without Benjamin. In fact, Judah doesn't mention Simeon at this point, or the prospects for his deliverance, or what it may be right to do for him. He focuses entirely on what it is pragmatic and necessary to do: the family needs food if they are to 'live and not die' (Jacob's words in Gen. 42:2). Not only Jacob, Judah himself and their 'little ones', but, by implication, the beloved Benjamin also needs to eat to live. And in prevailing on Jacob to see sense and to allow Benjamin to accompany the others, Judah demonstrates that he is ready to risk his own children in the enterprise. There is dignity and bravery as well as realism in Judah's words, which ultimately provokes a godly response in Jacob. The contrast with his role in relation to Joseph in Chapter 37 or Tamar in Chapter 38 could hardly be greater.

At first, Jacob has difficulty moving on from his fear and self pity. 'Why did you treat me so badly', he asks in verse 6, 'as to tell the man that you had another brother?' The grief expressed in Genesis 37:35 and 42:36 is still raw. At the end of this act of the drama, in verse 14, Jacob's last words are resigned: 'If I am bereaved, I am bereaved.' But immediately before that, the prayer expressed in verse 13 is more hopeful: 'May God Almighty grant you mercy before that man, so that he may send back your other brother and Benjamin.' This is the only reference to God on the lips of Jacob in the Joseph cycle, before the survival of Joseph is confirmed to him. It's also the only reference, admittedly pointedly not by name, to Simeon in the period of his captivity. The naming of Benjamin in contrast to 'your other brother' neatly reflects the respective value Jacob places on the lives of these two of his sons.

But this is nevertheless a prayer; and what Jacob prays for his sons is that they will experience the mercy of Almighty God. This is in fact the first reference to 'mercy' in the Bible. It is not used, let alone in connection with God, any earlier in the book of Genesis. But it will become one of the words most closely associated with God – a covenant word. Jacob, tenacious as he is by nature, may struggle to hold on to any lively sense of the mercy of God (verse 14); but instinctively he has identified not only what is needed in this situation, but what belongs to the nature of God. Jacob is speaking better than he knows.

Does Jacob himself trust in the mercy of God? His response to the disasters which have befallen him does not suggest so. If he is trusting in anything at this point, it would seem to be 'balm and honey, gum, resin, pistachio nuts, and almonds' (on which, compare Gen. 37:25) and what wealth the family can muster. Do the brothers trust in God's mercy? There's not much evidence of that either. But that doesn't in fact prevent God from acting in mercy. His gracious plan and purpose unfold in mercy whatever the capacity of his human creation to trust in it. In fact, nothing can prevent God from acting in mercy, because mercy is what comes naturally to him. He acts in mercy, not because we deserve it (we don't), not in view of our nature or character, but in view of his own: he is a God of mercy. This is good news for a church facing decline and disunity.

Act 2 (verses 15–34, Set in Egypt): A God of Grace

15 So the men took the present, and they took double the money with them, as well as Benjamin. Then they went on their way down to Egypt, and stood before Joseph. 16 When Joseph saw Benjamin with them, he said to the steward of his house, 'Bring the men into the house, and slaughter an animal and make ready, for the men are to dine with me at noon.'

17 The man did as Joseph said, and brought the men to Joseph's house. 18 Now the men were afraid because they were brought to Joseph's house, and they said, 'It is because of the money, replaced in our sacks the first time, that we have been brought in, so that he may have an opportunity to fall upon us, to make slaves of us and take our donkeys.' 19 So they went up to the steward of Joseph's house and spoke with him at the entrance to the house. 20 They said, 'Oh, my lord, we came down the first time to buy food; 21 and when we came to the lodging place we opened our sacks, and there was each one's money in the top of his sack, our money in full weight. So we have brought it back with us. 22 Moreover we have brought down with us additional money to buy food. We do not know who put our money in our sacks.' 23 He replied, 'Rest assured, do not be afraid; your God and the God of your father must have put treasure in your sacks for you; I received your money.' Then he brought Simeon out to them. 24 When the steward had brought the men into Joseph's house, and given them water, and they had washed their feet, and when he had given their donkeys fodder, 25 they made the present ready for Joseph's coming at noon, for they had heard that they would dine there.

26 When Joseph came home, they brought him the present that they had carried into the house, and bowed to the ground before him. 27 He inquired about their welfare, and said, 'Is your father well, the old man of whom you spoke? Is he still alive?' 28 They said, 'Your servant our father is well; he is still alive.' And they bowed their heads and did obeisance. 29 Then he looked up and saw his brother Benjamin, his mother's son, and said, 'Is this your youngest brother, of whom you spoke to me? God be gracious to you, my son!' 30 With that, Joseph hurried out, because he was overcome with affection for his brother, and he was about to weep. So he went into a private room and wept there. 31 Then he washed

his face and came out; and controlling himself he said, 'Serve the meal.' 32 They served him by himself, and them by themselves, and the Egyptians who ate with him by themselves, because the Egyptians could not eat with the Hebrews, for that is an abomination to the Egyptians. 33 When they were seated before him, the firstborn according to his birthright and the youngest according to his youth, the men looked at one another in amazement. 34 Portions were taken to them from Joseph's table, but Benjamin's portion was five times as much as any of theirs. So they drank and were merry with him.

The curtain falls on Act 1 at the end of verse 14. When it rises again in verse 15, the drama has moved from Canaan to Egypt, and the cast has changed: in place of Jacob, Joseph returns to centre stage. But unlike Act 1, Act 2 has more than one scene – three in fact. Joseph is present in scenes one (verses 15–16) and three (verses 26–34), but not in the middle scene, where the brothers are reunited with Simeon.

In Scene One then (verses 15–16), the brothers arrive in Egypt armed with their gift for Joseph and two lots of money to pay for grain – and complete with Benjamin too. When Joseph sees his younger brother, he immediately orders a steward to prepare a feast: the visitors are to eat with him in his own house at noon.

In Scene Two (verses 17–25), the steward escorts the brothers to Joseph's private apartments; but they are afraid. As with the discovery of the money in their sacks in the previous episode, they take this for a bad sign, not a good one. It can only be because he plans to exact a personal revenge from them for their failure to pay for the grain on their last visit, that he has ordered them to be taken to his house. There is no room in their fear for trust in God. In one of the many ironies in the story, it is left to the steward not only to reassure them when they seek to explain their circumstances to him, but also to remind them of God and to raise the possibility that, in the midst of all the chaos and distress, God might in fact be at work. 'Don't worry', he says to them. 'Your God and the God of your father must have put treasure in your sacks for you' (verse 23. Again, divine and human action is presented in concert). The Egyptian is reminding the Hebrews that it is in the nature of God to be generous.

Before the end of the scene, there follows what was presumably an awkward moment: Simeon is restored to them. He has no reason to know that it was the need for more food, rather than a concern for his welfare, which ultimately led to his brothers' return with Benjamin – but they do know. They know that they might never have come back, if the famine had eased (even if that was the result of their father's decision rather than their own).

Scene Three then opens with the first true fulfilment of Joseph's first dream (the one in 37:7) – all his brothers bow down to him (when they had bowed down to him in Genesis 42:6, Benjamin had not been present). Joseph's response, at least initially, is generous. He enquires after their welfare and Jacob's health. Again, they bow down – the second fulfilment of the dream. And then, in what is in one sense the climax of this Act, Joseph says to Benjamin, 'God be gracious to you, my son.' Given his love for Benjamin and the depth of his emotions at seeing him again, he must have been perilously close to saying, 'God be gracious to you, my brother.' Here it is Joseph's turn to speak better than he knows. If God is by nature merciful, he is also by nature gracious. And Joseph, holding the power in his relationship with his brothers, has a special responsibility to reflect the mercy and grace of God. And ironically, if up to this point in this episode, his generosity with his brothers has offered a glimpse of God's nature, in what follows Joseph's behaviour obscures it.

Up to verse 29, Joseph is generosity personified: in the feast he provides for his brothers, in his concern for their welfare and that of his father, in the blessing he pronounces on Benjamin. But from verse 30 to the end of the chapter, Joseph's actions are at odds with his prayer. He lacks the graciousness to which he refers. In verse 31, he is described as wanting to control himself; in fact he is seeking to control others too. In retreating to weep in private (the second of five connected weepings by Joseph in the presence of his brothers in Gen. 42–50, cf. 42:24; 43:2,14–15; 50:17); in eating apart from his brothers and in the Egyptian style; in the favouritism which commanded that Benjamin be given five times the serving that is offered to the others (like father, like son), Joseph fails to model the graciousness of God. Even when the chapter ends with the words, 'they drank and were merry with him', which might be taken to be a mark of Joseph's renewed generosity, it has to be borne in mind that in the following chapter, he will plant on them (to make it appear that they have stolen it from him) the cup from which he drinks.

Those with power can often struggle in this way, especially when there is a history of the kind that existed between Joseph and his brothers. Perhaps, for Joseph, old wounds are resurfacing. It is easy enough for him to grow in maturity in the absence of his family. So the spoilt brat of Chapter 37, develops into the model of integrity (Chapter 39), patience (Chapter 40), wisdom and action (Chapter 41). His virtues shine brightly against a family-free background. But the return of his brothers reveals his remaining flaws. Forgiveness and reconciliation are not easy or straightforward things. Perhaps immediate family often brings out the flaws in us. And perhaps the church family can do the same.

It's one thing to pray, as Joseph presumably prays in all sincerity, for someone else to know the grace of God. It's another thing to practise that grace ourselves.

But the wonder of the grace of God (in fact, the whole point about the grace of God) is that our failure does not deprive us of it. God does not withhold grace because we fail to reflect it in our lives. It would not be grace otherwise.

Conclusion

The challenge of Chapter 43 is to allow the character of God to shape our own. It is hard, especially in the face of famine and grief, to hold on to trust in the mercy of God and to behave mercifully ourselves. And it is hard, in times of bounty and power, to hold on to faith in the grace of God and to behave generously ourselves.

Chapter Nine

'God has found out'

(Genesis 44)

Introduction

Genesis 43 ends on what appears to be a most promising note: 'they (Joseph's brothers) drank and were merry with him.' On two levels this is a positive place for the brothers to be. At the level of their own awareness, it is almost too good to be true: not only does it appear that their journey will prove worthwhile in terms of both buying food and securing Simeon's release, but here they are eating and drinking with the lord of the land. What an unexpectedly welcome state of affairs. At the level of the reader's awareness, also, matters are fleetingly promising: here is Joseph, wining and dining his brothers and they are merry. This is a foretaste of a future reconciliation, at least. But forgiveness is not easily given or received and a further twist in the narrative is inevitable.

This episode, like many in the Joseph story, is made up of three clearly distinct scenes. In fact, the progression of the drama in Genesis 44 is neatly parallel to the previous act in Genesis 43:15–34: the 'cast' in the first scene (in verses 1–5; cf. 43:15–16) is Joseph and his steward with the brothers; in the second (verses 6 to 13; cf. 43:17–25), it is the steward and the brothers, without Joseph; and in the last (verses 14–34; cf. 43:26–34), Joseph himself and his brothers, without the steward.

Scene One: Joseph and the steward (verses 1–5)

1 Then he commanded the steward of his house, 'Fill the men's sacks with food, as much as they can carry, and put each man's money in the top of his sack. 2 Put my cup, the silver cup, in the top of the sack of the youngest, with his money for the grain.' And he did as Joseph told him. 3 As soon as the morning was light, the men were sent away with their donkeys. 4 When they had gone only a short distance from the city, Joseph said to his steward, 'Go, follow after the men; and when you overtake them, say to them, "Why have you returned evil for good? Why have you stolen my silver cup? 5 Is it not from this that my lord drinks? Does he not indeed use it for divination? You have done wrong in doing this."'

This latest episode in the story follows directly on the previous one: it is early on the morning after the night before (verse 3). It is not hard to imagine the brothers waking with banter, not quite able to believe their luck and teasing one another about any excess in their celebrating. As they gather themselves to set off for home, things could not be better. Simeon is free; Benjamin is safe; they still have the silver from their first visit; and after such a royal reception they are confident of securing the grain they need.

What the brothers do not know is that Joseph is plotting with his steward. He instructs him to fill their sacks to overflowing with food and discreetly to refund their money in the same way as before, by putting it in the neck of the sacks. But beyond that, he says, 'Put my cup, the silver cup, in the top of the sack of the youngest.' The proximity of Genesis 44:2 to Genesis 43:34 invites the reader to suppose this is the very cup with which Joseph had been drinking the night before (verse 5). Perhaps it is intended to appear as if Benjamin had stolen it off the banqueting table at the end of the meal.

The reader is bound to ask, 'Why?' Why is Joseph scheming like this? Have the brothers not in fact passed the 'test' he had set them? Was it really necessary for him to test them at all and is it really necessary to prolong the test any further? It is hard to avoid the impression that Joseph is playing cat and mouse with his brothers here, manipulating them in a misguided and mean-spirited way. Perhaps he is in fact, consciously or unconsciously, punishing them for what they did to him. The text offers no indication that Joseph sought God's guidance in these manoeuvrings. For individuals and institutions alike, it is really only possible to be punitive and mean-spirited, when God's guidance has not been sought. In church debates, certainly, a mean-spiritedness is a sure sign that it is time to seek the guidance of God again. In Joseph's case, his failure to seek God's will is emphasised by the fact that the cup he plants on his brother is 'used for divination' (verse 5). It may be implied that, since an instrument of an Egyptian art is involved, Joseph is acting outside the bounds of Hebrew piety here.

His brothers have only gone a short way from the city, when Joseph sends his steward to arrest them, accusing them of repaying his goodness (including perhaps the return of their silver) with evil.

Scene Two: The Steward and Joseph's Brothers (verses 6–13)

> 6 When he overtook them, he repeated these words to them. 7 They said to him, 'Why does my lord speak such words as these? Far be it from your servants that they should do such a thing! 8 Look, the money that we found at the top of our sacks, we brought back to you from the land of Canaan; why then would we steal silver or gold from your lord's house? 9 Should it be found with any one of your servants, let him die; moreover the rest of us will become my lord's slaves.' 10 He said, 'Even so; in accordance with your words, let it be: he with whom it is found shall become my slave, but the rest of you shall go free. 11 Then each one quickly lowered his sack to the ground, and each opened his sack. 12 He searched, beginning with the eldest and ending with the youngest; and the cup was found in Benjamin's sack. 13 At this they tore their clothes. Then each one loaded his donkey, and they returned to the city.

The consternation of the brothers, when they are confronted by the steward is palpable. They know themselves to be 'honest men' and seek to prove it by reminding the steward that when, on the equivalent journey on the previous occasion, they had found their money returned to them, they brought it back again so as not to profit from it dishonestly. They are so confident of their innocence that they make a vow almost as rash the one made by Jephthah (Judg. 11:31). 'Should [the cup] be found with any one of your servants, let him die,' they say. 'Moreover the rest of us will become my lord's slaves'.

The steward's reply is a nice example of ancient near eastern negotiation. When he says, 'Even so; in accordance with your words, let it be' (verse 10), it turns out that he does not mean 'What an excellent proposal. I agree to those terms.' He means, 'That is an unnecessarily harsh proposal and I reject it. I have an alternative suggestion to make.' For he then continues, 'The one on whom the cup is found shall become my slave, but the rest of you can go free.' There are other negotiations in the Bible, especially in the book of Genesis, which have this same flavour – such as the dialogue between Abraham and Ephron the Hittite in Genesis 23, over the purchase of the Cave of Machpelah as a burial place for Sarah. It transpires that the words of the two parties mean the exact opposite of their obvious sense (compare David negotiating with Ornan the Jebusite over the purchase of his threshing-floor as a site for an altar to the Lord in 1 Chronicles 21:22–25, especially verse 23).

So the brothers lower their sacks to the ground, and in age order (i.e., in the same order as they had sat at the banquet at which the cup supposedly went missing), beginning with Reuben, the oldest, they open them. Ten times, the result is the same and the brothers' sense of vindication grows: they know they have not committed any theft, and each open sack strengthens their conviction. But at the last, the cup is found with Benjamin. The brothers are distraught and tear their clothes. In biblical practice, this act is the response to a bereavement: the steward may have mitigated their proposed sentence, but Benjamin still stands to be enslaved and they know that that will be received as a mortal blow by their father.

So they load up their donkeys and return in trepidation to the city. The significance of that moment is not to be overlooked. According to the terms set by the steward, only the guilty party would be punished. The other brothers were free. Conceivably, they could have abandoned their brother to his fate, ridding themselves again of their father's favourite son. But they choose solidarity with Benjamin ahead of their own self-interest. Here is a model for the church family. It is the members who put solidarity (even with the party apparently in the wrong) before self-interest, who have discerned the way of God.

Scene Three: Joseph and his Brothers (verses 14–34)

14 Judah and his brothers came to Joseph's house while he was still there; and they fell to the ground before him. 15 Joseph said to them, 'What deed is this that you have done? Do you not know that one such as I can practice divination?' 16 And Judah said, 'What can we say to my lord? What can we speak? How can we clear ourselves? God has found out the guilt of your servants; here we are then, my lord's slaves, both we and also the one in whose possession the cup has been found.' 17 But he said, 'Far be it from me that I should do so! Only the one in whose possession the cup was found shall be my slave; but as for you, go up in peace to your father.' 18 Then Judah stepped up to him and said, 'O my lord, let your servant please speak a word in my lord's ears, and do not be angry with your servant; for you are like Pharaoh himself. 19 My lord asked his servants, saying, "Have you a father or a brother?" 20 And we said to my lord, "We have a father, an old man, and a young brother, the child of his old age. His brother is dead; he alone is left of his mother's children, and his father loves him" 21 Then you said to your servants, "Bring him down to me, so that I may set my eyes on him." 22 We said to my lord, "The boy cannot leave his father, for if he should leave his father, his father would die." 23 Then you said to your servants, "Unless your youngest brother comes down with you, you shall see my face no more." 24 When we went back to your servant my father we told him the words of my lord. 25 And when our father said, "Go again, buy us a little food," 26 we said, "We cannot go down. Only if our youngest brother goes with us, will we go down; for we cannot see the man's face unless our youngest brother is with us." 27 Then your servant my father said to us, "You know that my wife bore me two sons; 28 one left me, and I said, Surely he has

been torn to pieces; and I have never seen him since. 29 If you take this one also from me, and harm comes to him, you will bring down my gray hairs in sorrow to Sheol." 30 Now therefore, when I come to your servant my father and the boy is not with us, then, as his life is bound up in the boy's life, 31 when he sees that the boy is not with us, he will die; and your servants will bring down the gray hairs of your servant our father with sorrow to Sheol. 32 For your servant became surety for the boy to my father, saying, "If I do not bring him back to you, then I will bear the blame in the sight of my father all my life." 33 Now therefore, please let your servant remain as a slave to my lord in place of the boy; and let the boy go back with his brothers. 34 For how can I go back to my father if the boy is not with me? I fear to see the suffering that would come upon my father.'

The text states, a little surprisingly, that 'Judah and his brothers' returned to Joseph's house. The reader might have expected 'Reuben and his brothers' or even 'Benjamin and his brothers'. But through the course of the narrative, Judah has emerged as the brothers' natural leader (cf. 37:26; 43:3–9 – besides Chapter 38). And it will be Judah who acts as the spokesman for his brothers in this final scene, in as extended and moving a speech as the Bible has to offer.

Brought into the presence of Joseph, the brothers 'fall to the ground before him'. There is an even greater abasement here than in the previous chapters (42:6, 43:26–28) and a correspondingly greater fulfilment of Joseph's first dream (37:7).

Joseph challenges them not so much about their dishonesty or greed, but about their folly: 'How could you be so stupid. Did you not realise that a man like me can practise divination?'. Calvin is especially severe in his criticism of Joseph at this point: 'It was sinful for him to profess augury; for he vainly and unworthily transfers to imaginary deities the honour due only to divine grace.' Where previously he had been bold enough to correct Pharaoh, when the king ascribed to Joseph himself the power to interpret dreams, he now encourages the brothers to imagine that divination lies within his capacity. Of course, this is only part of a wider dissimulation: Joseph is playing a part – but all the while he exalts himself and humiliates his brothers.

It is Judah who steps forward. His confession bears close reading. There is no blaming of Benjamin. Indeed, his words leave room for the brothers' continued conviction that, as an individual, Benjamin is innocent of the theft. What Judah confesses is the corporate guilt of the brothers: as if the inexplicable appearance of the cup is an act of divine judgment. 'What can we say? How can we defend ourselves?', Judah says to Joseph, 'God has found out our guilt.' The ironies that run through the narrative are at their greatest here. The reader is in no doubt that Judah's words refer not to the theft of the cup, but to the sin the brothers had committed over twenty years previously against their brother – who now stands before them as their judge. He knows they are innocent of this crime, and he knows they are guilty of the other crime. They know (or they think they know) that he is convinced of their guilt in relation to this crime and that he is ignorant of the earlier one. Somehow the sin the brothers are not able to confess prevents them from defending themselves fully over the sin they have not committed.

When Judah reiterates (in spite of the assurances of the steward) that all the brothers are now to be regarded as Joseph's slaves, the reader knows that he and they have accepted the judgment of God. They do not understand how this has happened to them; but they believe they know why. Their sin has found them out at last. Perhaps, at some level, they are even relieved for the closure it brings.

Joseph maintains his charade and insists that only Benjamin need remain in Egypt: the other brothers are free to return home. But that is just what the brothers cannot contemplate and the prospect prompts Judah to speak again. His speech is, at sixteen verses, the longest single speech in the whole narrative (except for the rather odd and less narratively significant 'blessing of Jacob' in Chapter 49. The reformer Martin Luther regarded Judah's words as a model for Christian prayer.

First, tentatively, Judah seeks permission to speak (in verse 18). He is anxious not to inflame the situation further. Twice in the opening lines, Judah acknowledges himself as Joseph's servant and calls Joseph 'my lord'; he will use both terms again repeatedly in the following fifteen verses ('servant[s]' another ten times – even Jacob is 'your servant' in verses 24,27 and 30; 'lord' another three times).

Emboldened, Judah then reminds Joseph of the dialogue that took place between them on their first meeting (verses 19–29, cf. Gen. 42:13–38) – only this time the euphemism in relation to Joseph's fate is abandoned: he 'is dead' (verse 20). Judah's speech emphasises Jacob's advanced age and his vulnerability: 'if Benjamin were to leave his father, he would die.' If any harm comes to Benjamin, 'it would bring down [Jacob's] grey hairs in sorrow to Sheol'.

Finally, Judah makes his appeal. It is not exactly a plea for mercy, but for permission to suffer vicariously (verses 30–34). He informs Joseph that he has personally guaranteed Benjamin's safety on this journey and cannot afford to return home without him. A shift in language takes place at this point. Benjamin, who up until now has been 'the youngest brother', now becomes 'the boy' (the word comes just once in verses 18–29, but seven times in these last five verses). In fact, it is certain that Benjamin is a mature adult. His mother was dead before Joseph was 17, and he is now 39. In all probability, Benjamin is in his thirties – he is old enough at least to have fathered ten sons of his own (46:21)! The word is important however: it emphasises Benjamin's vulnerability, just as the repeated references to Jacob's great age emphasise his. Joseph, after all, had simply called the culprit 'the man' (verse 17, where NRSV has 'the one').

The climax of Judah's speech is his offer to remain in Egypt as a substitute for his brother. The man who was instrumental in selling one brother into slavery now offers to sell himself, in effect, to save another from the same fate. Similarly, he tells Joseph he could not now bear 'to see the suffering that would come upon [his father]' if Benjamin was harmed, whereas he had not hesitated to inflict the equivalent suffering where Joseph himself was concerned.

There is no explicit acknowledgment of the brothers guilt in relation to Joseph's fate – indeed, the reference to his 'death' in verse 20 can be read as their continued collusion in deceit. They do not know that Joseph is dead – but this is the story they have lived by for twenty two years. However, the acknowledgement of God's judgment and the real selflessness of Judah's offer (even in the face of his father's continued favouritism, compare verse 20 and the reference to Rachel as if she was Jacob's only wife in verse 27) demonstrate how much the brothers have changed in that time.

Judah's act of self-sacrifice is all the more impressive given the context of adversity. His family face famine and his father is frail. The temptation must have been strong to think, 'What I have, I hold.' The same dynamics beset the church. The tendency to behave in partisan ways is great when the future is bleak, and in such circumstances, self-sacrificial behaviour is correspondingly heroic.

The chapter ends without any resolution. The episode is the archetypal cliff-hanger. What will Joseph's response to this speech be?

Chapter Ten

'God has sent me before you'

(Genesis 45)

Introduction

One of the challenging aspects of the Joseph cycle is the way that the hand of God is discerned not so much in supernatural acts (in signs and wonders), but in the extraordinary timings of ordinary (or at least natural) events. For many of us, God discloses himself and his will as much in the coincidence as in the miracle, as much in retrospect as in prospect. Faith can be hard going under these circumstances: it would, we suppose, be so much easier (especially for a church facing decline or disunity) for God to make his will and purpose known in prospect not retrospect, and in signs and wonders not through ordinary life.

Episode Ten is the second great climax in the Joseph cycle, in some ways parallel to Episode Six (Gen 40:1–40). If that earlier episode was the climax of Joseph's story in terms of his relationship to Pharaoh, this one is the climax in terms of his relationship to his brothers. But it would be a mistake to characterise this episode (after the manner of the TV series, *Friends*) 'the one in which Joseph is recognised by his brothers' or 'the one in which Joseph reveals himself to his brothers'; it is as much 'the one in which Joseph comes to recognise God's hand at work' or 'the one in which God reveals his purpose to Joseph.'

The episode falls in three scenes: the first and longest scene is set in Egypt, and the cast consists of Joseph and his brothers; the second scene is also set in Egypt, and the cast is joined by

Pharaoh (or at least Pharaoh's voice); but the final scene is set in Canaan, as the brothers return to Jacob.

Scene One: Joseph and his Brothers (verses 1–15)

1 Then Joseph could no longer control himself before all those who stood by him, and he cried out, 'Send everyone away from me.' So no one stayed with him when Joseph made himself known to his brothers. 2 And he wept so loudly that the Egyptians heard it, and the household of Pharaoh heard it. 3 Joseph said to his brothers, 'I am Joseph. Is my father still alive?' But his brothers could not answer him, so dismayed were they at his presence. 4 Then Joseph said to his brothers, 'Come closer to me.' And they came closer. He said, 'I am your brother, Joseph, whom you sold into Egypt. 5 And now do not be distressed, or angry with yourselves, because you sold me here; for God sent me before you to preserve life. 6 For the famine has been in the land these two years; and there are five more years in which there will be neither ploughing nor harvest. 7 God sent me before you to preserve for you a remnant on earth, and to keep alive for you many survivors. 8 So it was not you who sent me here, but God; he has made me a father to Pharaoh, and lord of all his house and ruler over all the land of Egypt. 9 Hurry and go up to my father and say to him, "Thus says your son Joseph, God has made me lord of all Egypt; come down to me, do not delay. 10 You shall settle in the land of Goshen, and you shall be near me, you and your children and your children's children, as well as your flocks, your herds, and all that you have. 11 I will provide for you there – since there are five more years of famine to come – so that you and your household, and all that you have, will not come to poverty." 12 And now your eyes and the eyes of my brother Benjamin see that it is my own mouth that speaks to you. 13 You must tell my father how greatly I am honoured in Egypt, and all that you have seen. Hurry and bring my father down here.' 14 Then he fell upon his brother Benjamin's neck and wept, while Benjamin wept upon his neck. 15 And he kissed all his brothers and wept upon them; and after that his brothers talked with him.

Finally, Joseph puts aside his mask and his game-playing. Judah's speech is so extraordinarily apt that Joseph is overcome. It is clear that he is in fact overwhelmed: it is not that in some detached and objective manner, he now concludes that the brothers have indeed passed the test he had set them so that he can now entrust his true identity to them. Rather, it becomes clear that when Joseph seemed to be trying to manipulate and control his brothers, he was really seeking to manage and control himself. Judah's speech is so powerful, however, that it breaches his defences. Sensing that he is about to break down, he dismisses his staff (the interpreter, presumably, and perhaps the steward, as well as other more junior servants). Perhaps he did this to protect his brothers as much as himself: it becomes clear in the subsequent episodes that the arrival of his family was something Joseph felt needed to be negotiated with care. In any case, the reader knows the time has come for Joseph to reveal himself to his brothers: whereas previously he hid his tears from them (Gen. 42:24, 43:30), now he is prepared to weep in front of them.

Once they are alone, Joseph cannot control himself any longer and he bursts into sobs of tears: 'he wept so loudly that the Egyptians heard it and the household of Pharaoh heard it.' Who knows what the Egyptians made of what they were hearing? But in addition, what must the brothers have thought in the moment before he spoke? Judah has made an appeal, which is a matter of life and death, and with hearts in their mouths, the brothers are awaiting the response of the lord of the land. The last thing they expected was to find him bursting into tears on them. But perhaps in the tears they had just the first glimmer of recognition. He may have been weeping the last time they saw him.

Then Joseph speaks. Presumably – and this will not have reduced his brothers' bewilderment – he speaks to them in Hebrew (compare, in verse 12, 'It is my own mouth that speaks to you'). He doesn't work up to things gradually or break his news to them gently. He could hardly have come to the point more directly. 'I am Joseph', he says. 'Is my father still alive?' Personal pronouns are always loaded in the Joseph story. It is striking that he says, '*My* father', not '*Our* father'. He is not used to thinking of himself as one of twelve brothers. Besides, he needs to hear as 'Joseph' the news he has only previously been given as 'the lord of the land', that Jacob is alive and well.

His brothers are speechless – but not with joy. They are 'dismayed', it says. Here Joseph reaps what he has sown. Ever since they first encountered 'the lord of the land', the brothers have been subject to a confusing and disconcerting series of coincidences. Now in an instant all is clear: it is the hand of Joseph which has been toying with them. And what can his tears mean, except that he is deeply distressed by the betrayal which has been troubling their consciences and that he is now about to take his revenge?

What follows represents a moving invitation on Joseph's part to reconciliation. First, he invites them quite literally to come closer to himself. Then he invites them to enter emotionally into that physical closeness. He repeats his self-disclosure, with emphasis. He says not just 'I am Joseph', but 'I am *your brother*, Joseph.' He re-establishes the bond their betrayal had broken. And when he adds, 'whom you sold into Egypt', it is not preliminary to any reproach. Once he has named the deed, Joseph does not add any recriminations. On the contrary, he seeks to absolve and reassure them. 'Do not be angry with yourselves because you sold me here', he says, (he has heard their expressions of regret after all) 'for God sent me before you to preserve life' (verse 5). Presumably sensing his brothers might have difficulty hearing this message, Joseph repeats it: 'God sent me before you to preserve for you a remnant on earth' (verse 7). And a third time, with added emphasis, he says, 'It was not you who sent me here, but God' (verse 8).

Two things are worth noting about Joseph's understanding of what has happened to him. The first is that, while he sees God's action and human action happening in concert, he gives priority to the action of God. He can say, twice, 'you sold me' (verses 4 and 5); but also twice, 'God sent me' (verses 5 and 7); and once, 'It was not you who sent me here, but God' (verse 8). Joseph takes seriously enough the human agency; but ultimate responsibility for his situation is ascribed to God. Not only in times of prosperity and success or when blessings come, but in the face of adversity and trouble, Joseph sees the hand of God at work. This is what Christians mean when they speak of God's providence. We are subject to many adversities in the course of our lives – illnesses and bereavements, setbacks and disappointments. Some are 'mishaps'; others result from malice. But these things are themselves subject to the working of God: they have no power to remove us from his care or to thwart his good plan and purpose for us. On the contrary, these things (as much as prosperity and success) are the means by which God's will and purpose are fulfilled. This is as true in the experience of an institution as it is in the experience of an individual. This means that when a church finds itself confronted by decline and disunity, it should not assume too quickly that these things are contrary to the will of God. Nothing which befalls the church is outside the power and care of God; and he will deliver his church through it all. In the process, however, there may well be hard lessons for the church to learn. Of its present situation, therefore, the church needs to learn to say, to its detractors and adversaries: 'it was not you who sent me here, but God'.

Secondly, it is worth noting what Joseph understands as the reason for what has happened. Indeed, it is worth noting that it is instinctive to Joseph to make sense of his life in this way. It is not always possible – perhaps it is seldom possible – to find satisfying explanations for the bad things that happen to us (the kind of 'reasons' routinely offered in the face of sudden and unexpected bereavement for example are always inadequate and often inappropriate); but the attempt to find them is understandable. In Joseph's case, the connection he makes is with the promises of God to his father: he has been sent to Egypt 'to preserve life' (verse 5), 'to preserve for you a remnant on earth' (verse 7).

From verse 9, there is a shift in the focus of Joseph's words to his brothers. His concern in verses 4–8 is to convince them not only that he is who he says he is and that he means them no harm; his concern in verses 9–13 is to instruct them what they are to do next. He tells them to go and tell his father Jacob to come down to Egypt, so that he and his family may survive the famine. Having warned the brothers (in verse 6) that there are still five years of famine to come, he instructs them to pass the warning on to Jacob (verse 11). They are to assure their father that he, Joseph, will provide for him and for his children (the brothers themselves) and his children's children. The section begins, 'Hurry and go up to my father' (verse 8). It ends, 'Hurry and bring my father down here' (verse 13).

The scene ends as it began – in tears. Only now it is not just Joseph who is crying. First, he 'fell on his brother Benjamin's neck and wept, while Benjamin wept on his neck'; and then 'he kissed all his brothers and wept upon them.' Later in the story, it emerges that this reconciliation was only partial. But that was not apparent at the time and should not be allowed to detract from what took place. The kisses and tears signify a real restoration of relationships between estranged family members. And the scene closes with a delightfully realistic touch: 'after that, his brothers talked with him' (verse 15). Dumbstruck until now, the renewed tears create permission for them to speak. Besides, there was lots of catching up to do.

The text says, 'his brothers talked with him', but it is easier to imagine that Joseph talked with his brothers. They must have been desperate to know what happened after they first sold him into slavery and how he came to be 'lord of all the land'. They knew nothing, also, about Asenath, Manasseh and Ephraim (see Chapter 41:45–52). On the other hand, Joseph will have been pretty desperate himself, to hear how Jacob was and what the intervening years had brought for the family.

Scene Two: Pharaoh and Joseph's Brothers (verses 16–24)

16 When the report was heard in Pharaoh's house, 'Joseph's brothers have come,' Pharaoh and his servants were pleased. 17 Pharaoh said to Joseph, 'Say to your brothers, "Do this: load your animals and go back to the land of Canaan. 18 Take your father and your households and come to me, so that I may give you the best of the land of Egypt, and you may enjoy the fat of the land." 19 You are further charged to say, "Do this: take wagons from the land of Egypt for your little ones and for your wives, and bring your father, and come. 20 Give no thought to your possessions, for the best of all the land of Egypt is yours."' 21 The sons of Israel did so. Joseph gave them wagons according to the instruction of Pharaoh, and he gave them provisions for the journey. 22 To each one of them he gave a set of garments; but to Benjamin

he gave three hundred pieces of silver and five sets of garments. 23 To his father he sent the following: ten donkeys loaded with the good things of Egypt, and ten female donkeys loaded with grain, bread, and provision for his father on the journey. 24 Then he sent his brothers on their way, and as they were leaving he said to them, 'Do not quarrel along the way.'

There is a hint at the start of the first scene as well as in a later episode (Gen. 46:31–34), that the appearance of his family in Egypt was something sensitive for Joseph, a delicate matter to be handled with care. But when news reaches Pharaoh that Joseph's brothers have arrived, we are told, 'Pharaoh and his servants were pleased'.

Joseph has already taken the initiative, of course, to invite his father and wider family to come to Egypt. Indeed, he has already specified in his instructions to his brothers (verse 10), the region (Goshen – a fertile area close to the Nile Delta and to the border with Sinai) in which he expects them to settle. But quickly, the offer is endorsed by Pharaoh. He immediately reiterates that the brothers are to return to their father and bring him to Egypt, 'so that I may give you the best of the land of Egypt and you may enjoy the fat of the land'. It is worth noting, incidentally, that this is not the only time in the Bible that members of the people of God are honoured by the secular authorities, because they have proved themselves to be servants and agents of blessing for the community. This too is a model for the church to follow, not least in adverse times. 'Take wagons', Pharaoh goes on, 'Bring your father, and come'.

So when Joseph gives his brothers wagons and provisions for the journey, he is acting explicitly in accordance with Pharaoh's instructions. But when he gives Benjamin not just a single set of garments, such as the other brothers have received (verse 22), but 'three hundred pieces of silver and five sets of garments', he is acting on his own dubious initiative. Whatever lessons Joseph has learned from the events of the previous twenty-two years, the inadvisability of favouritism is not among them (notwithstanding the fact that Benjamin is Joseph's full brother, and the others only his half-brothers).

After providing also for Jacob, Joseph sends the brothers on their way. The scene ends with him calling cheerily after them as they depart, 'Don't quarrel along the way!' 'What?', it's almost possible to hear one of the brothers mutter, 'not even about the disproportionate gift you have given to Benjamin?' Tact was not the strong suit of the seventeen year old Joseph, and remains a weakness of the thirty-nine year old.

Scene Three: Jacob and Joseph's Brothers (verses 25–28)

> 25 So they went up out of Egypt and came to their father Jacob in the land of Canaan. 26 And they told him, 'Joseph is still alive! He is even ruler over all the land of Egypt.' He was stunned; he could not believe them. 27 But when they told him all the words of Joseph that he had said to them, and when he saw the wagons that Joseph had sent to carry him, the spirit of their father Jacob revived. 28 Israel said, 'Enough! My son Joseph is still alive. I must go and see him before I die.'

In the final scene of this episode, Jacob returns to the stage. The spotlight remains on him as much as on Joseph to the end of the whole narrative.

Just as Joseph had not beaten about the bush, when making himself known to the brothers, so they do not prevaricate when they are reunited with their father. 'Joseph is still alive!' they say, 'He is even ruler over all the land of Egypt.' It's likely the news was actually broken more gently than this – 'Dad, sit down. We've got something to tell you' – not just because Jacob was about one hundred and thirty years old at this stage, and because much has been made in the narrative of his great age and frailty; but because the brothers are bound to make a double confession here. Not only will they have to come clean about what they did to Joseph twenty-two years before; they will in the process have to admit to letting their father believe a lie for all that time (the final episode of the story makes it clear that Jacob did ultimately become aware of 'the crime of [the] brothers and the wrong they did in harming [Joseph]'; compare Gen. 50:17).

It is hardly surprising that Jacob, like the brothers before him, is stunned. Literally, the Hebrew says, 'His heart stopped.' But unlike them, what he feels is not dismay. He dare not believe his sons' report is true. What convinces him is not their report of all that Joseph had said to them, but the sight of the wagons Pharaoh had provided. As with Joseph's coat, it is the evidence of his eyes that Jacob believes.

At this, we read, 'Jacob's spirit revived.' For twenty-two years, he has been living in a state of quasi-death – paralysed by grief and despair. Now he has something to live for again. When he says, 'Enough!' (verse 28), he is calling time on his own emotional imprisonment. He still speaks of death ('My son Joseph is still alive. I must go and see him before I die'); but the vitality has returned to his voice. There is hope in it.

Chapter Eleven

'Do not be afraid to go down to Egypt'

(Genesis 46)

Introduction

Even if you live to see your grandchildren or great-grandchildren, it's unlikely that you will ever preside over a family of seventy or more members; even if the Lord appears to you in a dream and discloses to you his good will and purpose for your life, it's unlikely that he will promise to make your descendants into a great nation. And yet, the wonder of the Scriptures is that ordinary Christians like you and me can appropriately and legitimately identify with its characters – even its leading characters, its heroes. Indeed, we are encouraged to do so. We are invited to see our story in their story – their story as our story. We are invited to relate to their experience of walking with God and to hear in God's Word to them, his living Word to us. In a story which unfolded thousands of miles away and thousands of years ago, we are invited to find, in God's dealings with his people, a template for his dealings with us today. This is part of the function of the Bible: by the grace of God and the work of the Holy Spirit, believers are formed and shaped in the likeness of Christ at least partly through our exposure to the sacred text: as we read it and are drawn into its narrative, we grow not only in our knowledge of God but in our sense of being known by God.

For the first time since Genesis 38, Joseph himself is not central to an episode in 'the Joseph cycle'. Now that Joseph has been reconciled (at least superficially) to his brothers and his dreams have been largely fulfilled, the focus shifts onto his father Jacob. Jacob is by now an old man – as he himself puts it when he comes face to face with Pharaoh in the following episode, 'the years of [his] earthly sojourn have been one hundred and thirty' (cf. 45:9). The twenty-two years of Joseph's absence have taken their toll. His dramatic encounters with God (compare Gen. 32 and 35) are a distant memory. And now he is asked to make the arduous and spiritually counter-intuitive journey out of Canaan (the land promised to his father Isaac and his grandfather Abraham), in order to be reunited with his favourite son. Even in a time of continued famine, it must have seemed a terrible choice: remain in the land of promise and risk never seeing your favourite son again; or journey to Egypt for a reunion with the son and risk never seeing the Promised Land again. Christian faith does not relieve us of the need to make hard choices; often it seems to multiply them.

Chapter 46, like so many chapters in this narrative, falls neatly into three parts: in scene one (verses 1–7), there is an encounter between Jacob and God; in scene two (verses 8–27), there is an inventory of the members of Jacob's household who journey with him; and in scene three (verses 28–34), a second encounter, this time between Jacob and Joseph. Unlike Chapter 38, then, Joseph does at least make an appearance on stage in this episode, but only in the final scene.

Scene One: Jacob's Encounter with the God of Isaac (verses 1–7)

> 1 When Israel set out on his journey with all that he had and came to Beer-sheba, he offered sacrifices to the God of his father Isaac. 2 God spoke to Israel in visions of the night, and said, 'Jacob, Jacob.' And he said, 'Here I am.' 3 Then he said, 'I am God, the God of your father; do not be afraid to go down to Egypt, for I will make of you a great nation there. 4 I myself will go down with you to Egypt, and I will also bring you up again and Joseph's own hand shall close your eyes.' 5 Then Jacob set out from Beer-sheba; and the sons of Israel carried their father Jacob, their little ones,

and their wives, in the wagons that Pharaoh had sent to carry him. 6 They also took their livestock and the goods that they had acquired in the land of Canaan, and they came into Egypt, Jacob and all his offspring with him, 7 his sons, and his sons' sons with him, his daughters, and his sons' daughters; all his offspring he brought with him into Egypt.

When Jacob sets out on his journey with all his possessions and, at Beer-sheba 'offered sacrifices to [God]', it is the first act of religious observance attributed to him since the start of the Joseph cycle. Of course, he may have been honouring God with such sacrifices for the whole of the twenty-two years of his favourite son's absence; but if so, the text is silent about it, and the faithless self-pity into which he seems to have settled at the end of Chapters 37 and 42 would suggest not. But the news about his son has revived his soul, and Jacob picks up the pattern of his younger days, when he seems to have seen visions, met angels and offered worship to God at every turn (28:10–22; 31:1–13,53–54; 32:1,9–12, 22–32; 35:1–15).

This act of worship and subsequent vision were very necessary. In those younger days Jacob had received specific promises from God about his future, and specific instructions corresponding to them. At Bethel, for instance (just a day's journey from Beer-sheba to which he has now returned), he had heard the Lord say, 'The land on which you now lie, I will give to you and to your offspring, and your offspring shall be like the dust of the earth, and you shall spread abroad to the west and to the east and to the north and to the south; and all the families of the earth shall be blessed in you and your offspring' (Gen. 28:13–14). This three-fold promise (that God would provide him firstly with a land and secondly with numerous descendants, and – which is easy to overlook – that God would make him a blessing for all nations) is something Jacob inherited from his father and grandfather. The promise came first to Abraham in Genesis 12: land in verse 1, numerous descendants in verse 2, and blessing 'for all the families of the earth in verse 3 (compare 17:2–8; 18.18 and 22:17–18). The promise is renewed to Isaac in Genesis 26: land in verse 3, numerous descendants in verse 4 and blessing for 'all the nations of the earth' also in verse 4. But in that passage, the Lord's word to Isaac had begun, 'Do not go down to Egypt' (Gen. 26:2). Yet that is exactly what Jacob was now contemplating. The journey would be arduous and potentially hazardous, not least for a man of his advanced years. And it was possible that he was turning his back on the promises of God. So he offered a sacrifice to 'the God of his father, Isaac' (46:1). In fact, offering sacrifices to God at Beer-sheba is also something Jacob shares with his father and grandfather (compare Gen 21:31; 26:23).

'And God spoke to Israel in visions of the night.' We do not know the content of these visions, except for the word of the Lord spoken in them. We don't know what Jacob saw (perhaps he himself was not sure), only what he heard. This is frequently the way: God reveals to us not his inmost self, but his gracious word to us; not his essence, but what he is to us and for us. Consistently in the Bible, when God appears, he speaks.

'Jacob, Jacob', God said. And he said, 'Here I am.' As Joseph had replied to him in Genesis 37:13, so now Jacob replied to God: 'Here I am, at your service, ready and eager to do your bidding. What is it you want from me?' They are remarkable words in an old man, and especially one just roused from a stupor of grief and self-pity.

But all God wants on this occasion is to provide Jacob with reassurance. First, he identifies himself as 'the God of your father': that is, the God of Isaac to whom you have offered your sacrifices, and the God of the three-fold promise. Then, as so often in the Bible, God tells his human servant, 'Do not be afraid.' The words – or the synonymous words 'Do not fear' – occur on the lips, as it were, of God (that is, in a vision, or through an angel or a prophet), at least fifty times in the Bible. Hearing them is something else Jacob has in common with his father (Isaac in Gen. 26:24) and grandfather (Abraham in Gen. 15:1), as well as with, among others, Hagar (Gen. 21:17), Moses (Num. 21:34), Joshua (Josh. 11:6), Elijah (2 Kgs. 1:5), all Israel (frequently, not least in the prophecies of Isaiah, e.g., 41:10,13,14), the women at the empty tomb of Jesus (Mt. 28:5,10), Mary (Lk. 1:30), the shepherds at the birth of Jesus (Lk. 2:10), and the Apostle Paul (Acts 18:9, 27:24). Specifically, God tells Jacob not to be afraid to go down to Egypt: leaving the Promised Land will not annul the promise. Indeed, the journey is not only compatible with the

promise of God, it is the means by which the promise will be fulfilled. The point of the vision is to authorise Jacob's journey: 'Do
not be afraid to go down to Egypt, for I will make of you a great
nation there. I myself (the Hebrew is emphatic) will go down
with you to Egypt, and I will also bring you up again' (verses
3–4). In a region and at a time in which it was generally assumed
that a deity's power was territorially confined, this is a remarkable promise: even outside Canaan, God will continue to watch
over Jacob to protect and guide him.

In fact, Jacob will not return, except in death and in the person
of his descendants. But that doesn't trouble the narrator at all,
and certainly doesn't trouble Jacob: he is promised not only blessing in Egypt, but also the presence of God and the certainty of a
reunion with his son.

So Jacob sets off in renewed faith and hope and in the wagons
provided by Pharaoh. In an echo of an earlier journey he made,
to be reunited with his brother Esau (Gen. 32:22–23), Jacob trav-
els with all his belongings (his livestock and the goods he had
acquired in Canaan), with all his family (his sons and his sons'
sons; his daughters and his sons' daughters) – he sets off, so
infirm that he has to be carried by his sons, but reassured that he
will not die on the journey. When he and his family arrive in
Egypt, it will be as economic migrants.

Scene Two: An Inventory of Jacob's Family (verses 8–27)

> 8 Now these are the names of the Israelites, Jacob and his offspring,
> who came to Egypt. Reuben, Jacob's firstborn, 9 and the children of
> Reuben: Hanoch, Pallu, Hezron, and Carmi. 10 The children of
> Simeon: Jemuel, Jamin, Ohad, Jachin, Zohar, and Shaul, the son of a
> Canaanite woman. 11 The children of Levi: Gershon, Kohath, and
> Merari. 12 The children of Judah: Er, Onan, Shelah, Perez, and Zerah
> (but Er and Onan died in the land of Canaan); and the children of
> Perez were Hezron and Hamul. 13 The children of Issachar: Tola,
> Puvah, Jashub, and Shimron. 14 The children of Zebulun: Sered,
> Elon, and Jahleel 15 (these are the sons of Leah, whom she bore to
> Jacob in Paddan-aram, together with his daughter Dinah; in all his
> sons and his daughters numbered thirty-three).

16 The children of Gad: Ziphion, Haggi, Shuni, Ezbon, Eri, Arodi, and Areli. 17 The children of Asher: Imnah, Ishvah, Ishvi, Beriah, and their sister Serah. The children of Beriah: Heber and Malchiel 18 (these are the children of Zilpah, whom Laban gave to his daughter Leah; and these she bore to Jacob – sixteen persons). 19 The children of Jacob's wife Rachel: Joseph and Benjamin. 20 To Joseph in the land of Egypt were born Manasseh and Ephraim, whom Asenath daughter of Potiphera, priest of On, bore to him. 21 The children of Benjamin: Bela, Becher, Ashbel, Gera, Naaman, Ehi, Rosh, Muppim, Huppim, and Ard 22 (these are the children of Rachel, who were born to Jacob – fourteen persons in all).

23 The children of Dan: Hashum. 24 The children of Naphtali: Jahzeel, Guni, Jezer, and Shillem 25 (these are the children of Bilhah, whom Laban gave to his daughter Rachel, and these she bore to Jacob – seven persons in all).

26 All the persons belonging to Jacob who came into Egypt, who were his own offspring, not including the wives of his sons, were sixty–six persons in all. 27 The children of Joseph, who were born to him in Egypt, were two; all the persons of the house of Jacob who came into Egypt were seventy.

'Scene Two' isn't really a scene at all, as such. It's a list: an audit of those who made the journey with Jacob from Canaan to Egypt. But these verses serve in the drama as a scene, standing, in a sense, for the duration of the journey.

And of course the list has a certain value of its own. The three-fold promise of God to Abraham, Isaac and Jacob, was the promise of land, of numerous descendants and of blessing for all the nations of the earth. At this point in salvation history, it might seem as if the promise of land and perhaps also the promise of blessing for the world is as far from fulfilment as ever. But the inventory of Jacob's family provides some kind of assurance that at least in respect of the 'numerous descendants' there is already progress: God has blessed Jacob and the family of Abraham, within three generations, has multiplied considerably. Disregarding altogether any descendants of Ishmael or Esau, the chosen people are already a significant multitude of seventy or more.

The names and numbers in these verses, however, don't quite add up (though this doesn't seem to trouble the editor of the

narrative either!). Verses 9 to 15 list the sons and grandsons of
Leah (including Dinah, the only daughter named, perhaps on
account of her importance to the story in Gen. 34). Verse 15
specifically states: 'these are the sons of Leah, whom she bore to
Jacob in Paddan-aram, together with his daughter Dinah; in all
his sons and his daughters numbered thirty-three': but only the
one daughter is named and she takes the total named offspring to
thirty-four (if the deceased Er and Onan are included, or thirty-
two if not). Thirty-three is only the total number if Er and Onan
are included and Dinah excluded, which seems counter what the
text is saying. In verses 16–18, Jacob's children with Zilpah are
listed: sixteen of them according to the summary in verse 18. But
seventeen names are given, one of them a daughter, Serah.
Sixteen is only the total if Serah is excluded. There are no such
complications in verses 19–22: the text states that there were fourteen sons and grandsons born to Jacob with Rachel and fourteen
names are listed. Likewise in verses 23–25: seven sons and grandsons are said to have been born to Jacob with Bilhah, and seven
names are listed.

So the list includes seventy-two names; but the totals in verses
15,18,22 and 25 add up to seventy (presumably by excluding
Dinah and Serah). Verse 26 then states that excluding his sons'
wives (and, presumably, any surviving wives of his own), sixty-
six offspring made the journey to Egypt with Jacob. But that is a
hard figure to arrive at. If Er and Onan (who had died in Canaan)
and Joseph, Ephraim and Manasseh (who were already in Egypt)
are subtracted from the total, either sixty-five (if one works from
the totals provided in verses 15,18,22 and 25) or sixty-seven (if
one works from the total number of names listed) are left. In the
very next verse, moreover, it says, 'all the persons of the house of
Jacob who came into Egypt were seventy.' For those who like
their Bible facts neat and tidy, the matter is further complicated
by Stephen, who states in Acts 7:14 that 'Joseph sent and invited
his father Jacob and all his relatives to come to him, seventy-five
in all'!

But it misses the point to attempt to compute the figures exactly.
Plainly any miscalculation was not so problematic as to be eliminated in the editorial process by which the text has come to us: obvious as it is, it has been left to stand. Probably, the 'seventy' is, as

often in Scripture, an approximate and symbolic number, rather than one which is mathematically exact: ten times seven – the number of fullness, completion and perfection.

This central section is a reminder that 'the Joseph cycle' isn't really about an individual at all, but a family, a community. God deals with individuals, but he makes his home amongst and fulfils his purposes in and through a community. Perhaps there is also an echo here of the third part of the triple promise: that through this family, all the nations of the world are to be blessed. Even when God makes his home amongst and fulfils his purpose in and through a particular people, it is in order to bring blessing to all the nations of the earth. God's scope is never less than that. It is easy for the church of Jesus Christ to forget this, especially in times of adversity.

Scene Three: Jacob's Encounter with Joseph in Egypt (verses 28–33)

> 28 Israel sent Judah ahead to Joseph to lead the way before him into Goshen. When they came to the land of Goshen, 29 Joseph made ready his chariot and went up to meet his father Israel in Goshen. He presented himself to him, fell on his neck, and wept on his neck a good while. 30 Israel said to Joseph, 'I can die now, having seen for myself that you are still alive.' 31 Joseph said to his brothers and to his father's household, 'I will go up and tell Pharaoh, and will say to him, "My brothers and my father's household, who were in the land of Canaan, have come to me. 32 The men are shepherds, for they have been keepers of livestock; and they have brought their flocks, and their herds, and all that they have." 33 When Pharaoh calls you, and says, "What is your occupation?" 34 you shall say, "Your servants have been keepers of livestock from our youth even until now, both we and our ancestors" – in order that you may settle in the land of Goshen, because all shepherds are abhorrent to the Egyptians.'

The third and final scene in this episode is Jacob's long-awaited reunion with Joseph on his arrival in Egypt. Father and son have been separated for twenty-two years.

In the latter stages of the journey, Jacob sends Judah ahead to lead the way. The reason for this is not clear, but it marks the fourth and last significant act of leadership by Judah in these chapters. Judah's action is the cue for Joseph to set out in his (thoroughly Egyptian) chariot to meet his father – for Christian readers some kind of inversion of the parable of the Prodigal Son: in this case it is the son who is watching for the arrival of his father, and who goes rushing out to meet him while he is still some distance away. The reunion itself is full of emotion: the word 'neck' is repeated for emphasis: Joseph 'presented himself' to Jacob (or 'appeared to him' as if by some sort of divine epiphany), 'fell on his neck, and wept on his neck a good while' (verse 29). Jacob's speech is again reminiscent for Christian readers of the Song of Simeon (the *Nunc Dimittis*) on beholding the infant Jesus (Lk. 2:28–32): 'Now I can die in peace, for I have seen that you are alive.' Almost all Jacob's words since 37:35 have been words of death, but full of sorrow and despair. Here and in the chapters to follow, he still speaks of death, but his words are words of hope and thanksgiving. The tone has changed.

When Joseph speaks, it is to manoeuvre. Joseph, for all his growth in maturity and godliness, remains a born schemer. In this respect too, it is perhaps 'like father, like son'. Here he instructs his brothers and his father what they are to say when they come face to face with Pharaoh. Joseph is evidently anxious for some reason about how the occupation of his family will play out; and he is something of a control freak. He knows it is inevitable that Pharaoh will learn that his family are shepherds, because they have brought their flocks and herds with them (verse 32); but 'all shepherds are abhorrent to the Egyptians' (verse 34) and, born diplomat that he is, perhaps Joseph wishes to break this news to Pharaoh himself. He will say, 'The men are shepherds, for they have been keepers of livestock' (verse 32); so when Pharaoh calls his family into his presence and asks them, 'What is your occupation?', he will be prepared for them to say, 'Your servants have been keepers of livestock.' His aim is to ensure that his family are settled in Goshen and ultimately he succeeds in his goal. But perhaps less manoeuvring on his part and more trust in God's grace would have been appropriate.

Chapter Twelve

'Jacob blessed Pharaoh'

(Genesis 47)

Introduction

Ours is a culture which doesn't really know how to speak about death. To name death is generally regarded, superstitiously, as to invite it. People tend not to speak about making wills or funeral plans (either their own or someone else's), out of a sense that it somehow makes death more likely or imminent. We avoid talk about death despite knowing perfectly well that we will die. We confine death and dead bodies where possible to private places, ushering people out of their homes (the place where death most often occurred in previous generations) into hospitals and hospices. We try to protect our children from the reality of death – discouraging them, for example, from attending funerals. In previous generations they were more likely to be found playing chase around the deceased close relative laid out overnight in the coffin in the front room.

This superstitious fearfulness is not the response of faith. Death need not be a taboo for Christians. In Jesus' words, the God of Abraham, Isaac and Jacob 'is not the God of the dead, but of the living' (Mk. 12:27 and parallels). For those who trust in God, the challenge is to embrace death as a part of life and to speak of it without fear and with hope. Jacob offers an example in this episode of the Joseph story.

There are three scenes to this episode (although they are almost three separate episodes really): in Scene One (verses 1–12), Jacob meets Pharaoh and blesses him; in Scene Two (verses

13–26), Joseph ruthlessly manages the famine in Egypt; and in the final scene (verses 27–31), Jacob prepares to die, without fear.

Scene One: Joseph Manages his Family's Audience with Pharaoh (verses 1–12)

> 1 So Joseph went and told Pharaoh, 'My father and my brothers, with their flocks and herds and all that they possess, have come from the land of Canaan; they are now in the land of Goshen.' 2 From among his brothers he took five men and presented them to Pharaoh. 3 Pharaoh said to his brothers, 'What is your occupation?' And they said to Pharaoh, 'Your servants are shepherds, as our ancestors were.' 4 They said to Pharaoh, 'We have come to reside as aliens in the land; for there is no pasture for your servants' flocks because the famine is severe in the land of Canaan. Now, we ask you, let your servants settle in the land of Goshen.' 5 Then Pharaoh said to Joseph, 'Your father and your brothers have come to you. 6 The land of Egypt is before you; settle your father and your brothers in the best part of the land; let them live in the land of Goshen; and if you know that there are capable men among them, put them in charge of my livestock.' 7 Then Joseph brought in his father Jacob, and presented him before Pharaoh, and Jacob blessed Pharaoh. 8 Pharaoh said to Jacob, 'How many are the years of your life?' 9 Jacob said to Pharaoh, 'The years of my earthly sojourn are one hundred thirty; few and hard have been the years of my life. They do not compare with the years of the life of my ancestors during their long sojourn.' 10 Then Jacob blessed Pharaoh, and went out from the presence of Pharaoh. 11 Joseph settled his father and his brothers, and granted them a holding in the land of Egypt, in the best part of the land, in the land of Rameses, as Pharaoh had instructed. 12 And Joseph provided his father, his brothers, and all his father's household with food, according to the number of their dependents.

As we have seen, Joseph was something of a control freak. He was evidently anxious about the reception of his family by Pharaoh and had clear views about how that encounter might best be managed. His sensitivity is around the fact that his family are shepherds, and 'all shepherds are abhorrent to the Egyptians' (Gen. 46:34). So, at the conclusion of the previous episode, Joseph had proposed first, that he himself would go up to Pharaoh to prepare the way (Gen 46:31); and then, when Pharaoh summoned the brothers and enquired about their occupation, that his brothers should stick to a response he had scripted.

Events unfold pretty much according to plan. Joseph duly meets with Pharaoh to prepare the way. In fact, when he speaks to Pharaoh he appears to omit the very fact – that his brothers are shepherds – it had seemed so important to mention (Gen. 46:32), although he is careful to establish that they are presently in Goshen. He then takes a further step to manage the situation. He hand picks five of his brothers and presents them to Pharaoh. One wonders which five he picked, and which six he overlooked and why? Benjamin was surely included; perhaps also Judah and Reuben. It seems unlikely that Joseph just chose the oldest five or some random combination. It wouldn't be a total surprise if the five did not include Gad and Asher, Dan and Naphtali – the sons of Bilhah and Zilpah, whose sulky assistant Joseph had been as a teenager (Gen. 37:2). In fact which brothers were selected and which were not and for what reason – and how the brothers who were not selected felt about being overlooked – may not matter greatly; but on the other hand, it is part of the context against which, in the final episode, the residual distrust of the brothers towards Joseph is to be understood. At any rate, Joseph was scheming once more.

Sure enough, as Joseph has anticipated or designed, Pharaoh asks the brothers about their occupation (verse 3). The brothers reply that they are shepherds (it's not quite clear whether or not in Genesis 46:32,34, when he tutored his brothers in advance of this interview, Joseph meant that he would use the word 'shepherds' and they should avoid it; or whether the terms 'keepers of livestock' and 'shepherds' were effectively synonyms). They request Pharaoh's permission first to sojourn and then to settle in Goshen (verse 4), which is granted. Not only so, but Pharaoh tells Joseph that 'if there are capable men' among his brothers (such as Joseph's handpicked five, one might think), he is to put them in charge of Pharaoh's livestock.

Then, with the delicate negotiations out of the way, Joseph presents his father Jacob to Pharaoh and Jacob blesses him (verse 7). Once again, the point is repeated for emphasis (verse 10). Presumably, there is a reference here to the promise Jacob has received from God. As we have seen, it was a three-part promise (Gen. 28:13–14): God promised first to give him a land, second to give him a numerous family and thirdly also to make him a means of blessing for all the nations of the world. The same three-fold promise was made to his father Isaac (Gen. 26:3–4) and to his grandfather Abraham (Gen. 12:1–3).

The 'scandal of particularity' – that God should choose a particular people to be his own, to bless them with land and descendants – is most scandalous when its ultimate purpose (that through them all the nations of the world should be blessed) is forgotten. Unfortunately, it is precisely this third part of the promise to the Patriarchs which it is most easy to overlook or forget. When God elects to makes himself known, the gift always carries a responsibility: those he blesses are always blessed in order that they might be a blessing to others. Here, as Jacob blesses Pharaoh, there is a preliminary fulfilment of the third part in that promise. As Jacob blesses Pharaoh, Israel blesses Egypt – a symbol of all the nations of the world.

When he first blesses Pharaoh, Jacob is asked his age. He replies by saying not just that he has lived one hundred and thirty years – a length of life which does not compare, he says, with that of his ancestors (the ages of the patriarchs in Genesis and their ancestors essentially decline over time, so that the book ends with the human lifespan at almost a 'normal' length), but that his life has been 'hard'. It is then that he blesses Pharaoh a second time. The link to both his age and his hardships is not to be missed: by the grace of God, both adversity and long experience often increase a person's capacity to be a blessing to others.

The scene closes with a note that Joseph settled his father and his brothers in 'the best of the land of Egypt' and provided food for them and for their descendants. This is in accordance with Pharaoh's instructions (verse 12) but also in accordance with Joseph's own promise (Gen 45:10, 'settle'; 45:11, 'provide').

Scene Two: Joseph Manages the Famine (verses 13–26)

13 Now there was no food in all the land, for the famine was very severe. The land of Egypt and the land of Canaan languished because of the famine. 14 Joseph collected all the money to be found in the land of Egypt and in the land of Canaan, in exchange for the grain that they bought; and Joseph brought the money into Pharaoh's house. 15 When the money from the land of Egypt and from the land of Canaan was spent, all the Egyptians came to Joseph, and said, 'Give us food! Why should we die before your eyes? For our money is gone.' 16 And Joseph answered, 'Give me your livestock, and I will give you food in exchange for your livestock, if your money is gone.' 17 So they brought their livestock to Joseph; and Joseph gave them food in exchange for the horses, the flocks, the herds, and the donkeys. That year he supplied them with food in exchange for all their livestock. 18 When that year was ended, they came to him the following year, and said to him, 'We can not hide from my lord that our money is all spent; and the herds of cattle are my lord's. There is nothing left in the sight of my lord but our bodies and our lands. 19 Shall we die before your eyes, both we and our land? Buy us and our land in exchange for food. We with our land will become slaves to Pharaoh; just give us seed, so that we may live and not die, and that the land may not become desolate.' 20 So Joseph bought all the land of Egypt for Pharaoh. All the Egyptians sold their fields, because the famine was severe upon them; and the land became Pharaoh's. 21 As for the people, he made slaves of them from one end of Egypt to the other. 22 Only the land of the priests he did not buy; for the priests had a fixed allowance from Pharaoh, and lived on the allowance that Pharaoh gave them; therefore they did not sell their land. 23 Then Joseph said to the people, 'Now that I have this day bought you and your land for Pharaoh, here is seed for you; sow the land. 24 And at the harvests you shall give one-fifth to Pharaoh, and four-fifths shall be your own, as seed for the field and as food for yourselves and your households, and as food for your little ones.' 25 They said, 'You have saved our lives; may it please my lord, we will be slaves to Pharaoh.' 26 So Joseph made it a statute concerning the land of Egypt, and it stands to this day, that Pharaoh should have the fifth. The land of the priests alone did not become Pharaoh's.

For the first time since Chapter 41, the focus of the narrative reverts from Joseph's role in relation to his family to his role in relation to the people of Egypt. And disconcertingly, in this central scene of the episode Joseph is presented as an agent of oppression. Here too, his character as a controller and manipulator of others is emphasised. Admittedly, the text may be read as a celebration of Joseph's shrewd administration. But for sensitive readers of the Bible, alert to God's bias to those who are most marginalised and powerless, the depiction of Joseph in these verses is not an attractive one.

The famine is severe, not just in Egypt but (to confirm the wisdom of Jacob's decision to move his family) in Canaan too. But it is not just visitors like Joseph's brothers who are now required to buy food: even the Egyptians are now having to do so – and it is Joseph who is collecting the money and depositing it 'in Pharaoh's house'.

Then, however, their money runs out (verse 15) and a two-stage escalation follows in the Egyptians' distress. First (in verses 16 and 17), Joseph proposes that the Egyptians exchange their cattle for food. The people of Egypt agree (they fear that they will otherwise die); and this is the pattern for a year. Then the following year, when not just all the money but also all the livestock has been handed over to Joseph, the people propose that they exchange for food the only resources they have left to offer: their land and their own bodies (literally, 'corpses'; verses 18 to 21). The text carefully specifies that the Egyptians sold all their fields, so that the land became Pharaoh's; and that Joseph made slaves of the people, 'from one end of Egypt to the other' (verse 21). Despite the fulsome gratitude the people apparently feel towards Joseph as their saviour (verse 25), the inescapable impression created in these verses is of exploitation on Joseph's part. The serfdom to which the people of Egypt are reduced makes a sobering background to the later story of the Israelite Exodus.

There is one exception: 'the land of the priests he did not buy' (verse 22), because they had a special allowance from Pharaoh which enabled them to purchase as much food as they needed. 'The land of the priests alone did not become Pharaoh's' (verse 26). But of course, Joseph had a personal interest here: he had married into a priestly family – his wife Asaneth was the daughter of

Potiphera, the priest of On (Gen. 40:45). The fact that the priests enjoyed a privileged exemption from the general enslavement only adds to the distasteful depiction of Joseph in these verses. The other exemption, of course, is Joseph's own large family for whom the last verse of the previous scene (verse 12) has told us he fully provided with food. So while the mass of the Egyptian population is suffering acute distress, Jacob's Hebrew family and his Egyptian relatives are protected and provided for. At this point, there is no sign of any blessing for the Egyptians through the Israelites. It may be no coincidence that Genesis 47 is the first chapter since the opening two chapters (Gen. 37 and 38) in the Joseph story in which there is no reference to God. Joseph's ruthlessness towards the poorest in Egypt has the effect of marginalising all reference to God in the text.

Scene Three: Jacob Nears Death (verses 27–31)

27 Thus Israel settled in the land of Egypt, in the region of Goshen; and they gained possessions in it, and were fruitful and multiplied exceedingly. 28 Jacob lived in the land of Egypt seventeen years; so the days of Jacob, the years of his life, were one hundred forty-seven years. 29 When the time of Israel's death drew near, he called his son Joseph and said to him, 'If I have found favour with you, put your hand under my thigh and promise to deal loyally and truly with me. Do not bury me in Egypt. 30 When I lie down with my ancestors, carry me out of Egypt and bury me in their burial place.' He answered, 'I will do as you have said.' 31 And he said, 'Swear to me'; and he swore to him. Then Israel bowed himself on the head of his bed.

In the final scene of this episode, the focus shifts back again to Jacob and to Joseph's role in relation to his family. 'Israel settled in the land of Egypt . . . and [his family was] fruitful and multiplied exceedingly.' Through the book of Genesis, from the programmatic Chapter 1 verse 28, the words 'be fruitful and multiply' mark the outworking of God's blessing. At the 'recreation' after the flood, Noah is exhorted 'to be fruitful and multiply on the earth' (Gen. 8:17; compare 9:1,7). God then promises Abraham

(Gen. 17:6,20) and Isaac (Gen. 26:22; 28:3) that he will make them fruitful, before exhorting Jacob, in exactly the words used in this passage to 'be fruitful and multiply' (Gen. 35:11). Only economic reasons are ever given in the narrative for Jacob's migration from Canaan to Egypt, but here it is made clear that the step furthers God's purpose for his covenant people. Jacob's family is fruitful and multiplies into the numerous nation it is destined to become.

Jacob 'lived in the land of Egypt for seventeen years' (verse 28). This means, of course, that he spent exactly as long with Joseph in Egypt as he had spent with him in Canaan. A medieval Jewish commentator observes, 'just as Joseph was in the lap of Jacob seventeen years, Jacob was in the lap of Joseph seventeen years.'

The blessing which Jacob's family have enjoyed in that seventeen years presents a temptation similar to the one that faced Joseph when he entered the service of Pharaoh: if the Israelites are flourishing so fully in Goshen, why would they ever aspire to return to the land God had promised them? So as he nears his death, Jacob elicits a promise from his favourite son, still acting as if he was the oldest. He exacts a promise from Joseph not to bury him in Egypt. He knows he will not see his family established in the promised land; but before he dies, he wishes to do everything he can to anchor his children in the promise. Goshen can be a place of sojourn – even a place of blessing – but never Israel's home.

Chapter Thirteen

'Blessings of the Deep
that lies beneath'

(Genesis 48:1 – 49:28)

Introduction

'Blessing' does not have robust connotations in twenty-first century western cultures. When someone sneezes, we may hear a 'Bless you!' When something cute (or unexpectedly kind) happens, we may hear an 'Ah, bless!' When there is gratitude to express, we may occasionally hear a 'Well, bless his cotton socks' (though there's a patronising note in the phrase). None of these uses of the word conveys anything like the biblical weight of 'bless'. We might get closer to the Scriptural use when we hear a person described as 'blessed with good looks' – which at least implies God-given gifts – or when we hear an event described as 'a blessing in disguise' – which perhaps implies the providence of God.

But 'blessing' is a key category in the book of Genesis as a whole, and in the Joseph cycle in particular. We have already noted that it was God's purpose, in choosing and blessing Jacob, for Israel to be a blessing to the nations of the world. So it is entirely appropriate, that the last act of Jacob's life is to bless.

The death of which Jacob has spoken since Joseph was taken from him thirty-nine years before (Gen. 37:35) is now imminent for him. Throughout the Joseph cycle, his death has preoccupied him. He almost never opens his mouth without referring to it (cf., Gen 42:38; 45:28; 46:30; 47:29–30). But where at times in the story it seemed he must die cursing, circumstances have conspired to enable him to die pronouncing a blessing.

This penultimate episode of the Joseph cycle falls into two parts. In Scene One (Gen. 48:1–22), Jacob blesses the two sons of Joseph, Ephraim and Manasseh; in Scene Two (Gen. 49:1–28), he blesses his own twelve sons. The first scene, however, falls into three parts.

Scene One: The Blessing of Manasseh and Ephraim (Genesis 48:1–22)

a) Jacob's words to Joseph (verses 1–12)

> 1 After this Joseph was told, 'Your father is ill.' So he took with him his two sons, Manasseh and Ephraim. 2 When Jacob was told, 'Your son Joseph has come to you,' he summoned his strength and sat up in bed. 3 And Jacob said to Joseph, 'God Almighty appeared to me at Luz in the land of Canaan, and he blessed me, 4 and said to me, "I am going to make you fruitful and increase your numbers; I will make of you a company of peoples, and will give this land to your offspring after you for a perpetual holding." 5 Therefore your two sons, who were born to you in the land of Egypt before I came to you in Egypt, are now mine; Ephraim and Manasseh shall be mine, just as Reuben and Simeon are. 6 As for the offspring born to you after them, they shall be yours. They shall be recorded under the names of their brothers with regard to their inheritance. 7 For when I came from Paddan, Rachel, alas, died in the land of Canaan on the way, while there was still some distance to go to Ephrath; and I buried her there on the way to Ephrath' (that is, Bethlehem). 8 When Israel saw Joseph's sons, he said, 'Who are these?' 9 Joseph said to his father, 'They are my sons, whom God has given me here.' And he said, 'Bring them to me, please, that I may bless them.' 10 Now the eyes of Israel were dim with age, and he could not see well. So Joseph brought them near him; and he kissed them and embraced them. 11 Israel said to Joseph, 'I did not expect to see your face; and here God has let me see your children also.' 12 Then Joseph removed them from his father's knees, and he bowed himself with his face to the earth.

The penultimate episode in the Joseph cycle begins with the news reaching Joseph that his father is ill. This implies some distance between father and son. Jacob may be settled in Goshen with his family, while Joseph remains at Pharaoh's court, occupied with the administration of the kingdom.

But Joseph makes the journey to see his father, taking with him his own two sons, Manasseh and Ephraim, whose only contribution to the Joseph cycle this is (and who are carefully named in order of their births, compare Gen. 41:50–57). It is highly significant that, with his father's death impending, Joseph takes his two sons with him. It demonstrates what Joseph – who had given them Hebrew names – most wants for his boys. He himself is able to give them most things that a father might wish to be able to give his children: wealth, education, social status. They are, after all, second generation immigrants to Egypt and could assimilate, probably into a priestly caste, if they chose. But only Jacob can give them an enduring place among God's people, and it is this that Joseph most wants for them. Joseph knows that his father's deathbed is the appropriate place to seek it.

When Jacob hears that Joseph has come to see him, he rouses himself from his sickbed. The first reference to 'blessing' in this episode is to the blessing that Jacob himself received from God (verse 3). His capacity to bless others and to be a blessing to others is derived from this blessing he himself has received. But in recounting his experience, Jacob abbreviates it in the predictable way. He recalls that God promised to make him 'a company of peoples' and to give him Canaan 'for a perpetual holding'. But he neglects to mention that God's ultimate intention was for Jacob and his descendants to be a blessing 'to the nations of the world'.

Nevertheless, Jacob sees the importance of embracing Manasseh and Ephraim and confirming their place in the people of God. 'Ephraim and Manasseh shall be mine', he says, 'as Reuben and Simeon (his first-and second-born) are mine' (verse 5). But when he is actually faced with them, Jacob asks, 'Who are these?', and Joseph replies, 'They are my sons, whom God has given me.' Perhaps, in the light of his own experience, Jacob wanted to be sure that there were no impostors on the scene (Gen. 27). After all, just as his father Isaac's had been, Jacob's 'eyes were dim with age and he could not see well.' But he requests Joseph to bring his sons forward, so that he can bless them.

Jacob had not expected to see Joseph again, let alone Joseph's children. Their father removes them, then, from Jacob's knees in anticipation of his blessing; they are after all only small children – Joseph has been married to Asenath for just nine years (it is the second year of famine, after the seven years of plenty).

b) *Jacob's words to Manasseh and Ephriam (verses 13–20)*

> 13 Joseph took them both, Ephraim in his right hand toward Israel's left, and Manasseh in his left hand toward Israel's right, and brought them near him. 14 But Israel stretched out his right hand and laid it on the head of Ephraim, who was the younger, and his left hand on the head of Manasseh, crossing his hands, for Manasseh was the firstborn. 15 He blessed Joseph, and said, 'The God before whom my ancestors Abraham and Isaac walked, the God who has been my shepherd all my life to this day, 16 the angel who has redeemed me from all harm, bless the boys; and in them let my name be perpetuated, and the name of my ancestors Abraham and Isaac; and let them grow into a multitude on the earth.' 17 When Joseph saw that his father laid his right hand on the head of Ephraim, it displeased him; so he took his father's hand, to remove it from Ephraim's head to Manasseh's head. 18 Joseph said to his father, 'Not so, my father! Since this one is the firstborn, put your right hand on his head.' 19 But his father refused, and said, 'I know, my son, I know; he also shall become a people, and he also shall be great. Nevertheless his younger brother shall be greater than he, and his offspring shall become a multitude of nations.' 20 So he blessed them that day, saying, 'By you Israel will invoke blessings, saying, "God make you like Ephraim and like Manasseh."' So he put Ephraim ahead of Manasseh.

Then Joseph presented his sons to his father for his blessing: ever the careful manager, he steered Ephraim (the younger son) towards Jacob's left hand and Manasseh (the older) towards Jacob's right. But Jacob crossed his hands, to lay his right hand (the pre-eminent hand) on Ephraim's head and his left (the lesser) on Manasseh. Jacob knew a thing or two about the limits of birth seniority in determining priority with God. He himself had displaced the older Esau (Gen. 27), and his father Isaac was not literally the 'firstborn' either (Gen. 16:15–16; 21:2–3).

First, Jacob blessed Joseph; or at least, that's what the text at first says. When Jacob recalls God's dealings with him, his troubles (with Esau and Laban) and sorrows (over Rachel and Joseph) – not to mention his own character as a cheat and a deceiver – slip his mind. He recalls only the good things. As a shepherd, the father of a family of shepherds, he recalls 'the God who has been my shepherd to this day' (verse 15). Although he had told Pharaoh his one hundred and thirty years had been 'hard', he recalls 'the angel who has redeemed me from all harm' (compare Gen. 31:11; 32:2).

Then, without warning, he proceeded to bless the boys (verse 16) – praying that as the true descendants of Abraham and Isaac, they might 'grow into a multitude in the earth'. At once, Joseph interjected. He didn't only speak, to point out to his father which son was his firstborn, he physically 'took his father's hand to remove it from Ephraim's head' (verse 17). But Jacob insists: Manasseh will 'become a people', but Ephraim's descendants will 'become a multitude of nations' (verse 19). 'So he blessed them that day, saying, "By you Israel will invoke blessings, saying, 'God make you like Ephraim and Manasseh'".' So, the text concludes, he 'put Ephraim before Manasseh.' In fact, he had already done so in speaking of them in verse 5.

c) Jacob's words to Joseph (verses 21–22)

> 21 Then Israel said to Joseph, 'I am about to die, but God will be with you and will bring you again to the land of your ancestors. 22 I now give to you one portion more than to your brothers, the portion that I took from the hand of the Amorites with my sword and with my bow.'

But Jacob's concern is not just to include his grandsons in God's promise that his descendants would become numerous; he wanted also to include them in the promise of a land. So this first scene closes with Jacob apparently reasserting the favouritism with which the whole Joseph cycle began. It concludes with Jacob saying to Joseph, 'I give to you one more portion than to your brothers' (verse 22).

Scene Two: The Blessing of Jacob's Twelve Sons (Genesis 49.1–28)

1 Then Jacob called his sons, and said: 'Gather around, that I may tell you what will happen to you in days to come. 2 Assemble and hear, O sons of Jacob; listen to Israel your father.

3 Reuben, you are my firstborn, my might and the first fruits of my vigour, excelling in rank and excelling in power. 4 Unstable as water, you shall no longer excel because you went up onto your father's bed; then you defiled it – you went up onto my couch!

5 Simeon and Levi are brothers; weapons of violence are their swords. 6 May I never come into their council; may I not be joined to their company – for in their anger they killed men, and at their whim they hamstrung oxen. 7 Cursed be their anger, for it is fierce, and their wrath, for it is cruel! I will divide them in Jacob, and scatter them in Israel.

8 Judah, your brothers shall praise you; your hand shall be on the neck of your enemies; your father's sons shall bow down before you. 9 Judah is a lion's whelp; from the prey, my son, you have gone up. He crouches down, he stretches out like a lion, like a lioness – who dares rouse him up? 10 The sceptre shall not depart from Judah, nor the ruler's staff from between his feet, until tribute comes to him; and the obedience of the peoples is his. 11 Binding his foal to the vine and his donkey's colt to the choice vine, he washes his garments in wine and his robe in the blood of grapes; 12 his eyes are darker than wine, and his teeth whiter than milk.

13 Zebulun shall settle at the shore of the sea; he shall be a haven for ships, and his border shall be at Sidon.

14 Issachar is a strong donkey, lying down between the sheepfolds; 15 he saw that a resting place was good, and that the land was pleasant; so he bowed his shoulder to the burden, and became a slave at forced labour.

16 Dan shall judge his people as one of the tribes of Israel. 17 Dan shall be a snake by the roadside, a viper along the path, that bites the horse's heels so that its rider falls backward. 18 I wait for your salvation, O LORD.

19 Gad shall be raided by raiders, but he shall raid at their heels. 20 Asher's food shall be rich, and he shall provide royal delicacies. 21 Naphtali is a doe let loose that bears lovely fawns.

22 Joseph is a fruitful bough, a fruitful bough by a spring; his branches run over the wall. 23 The archers fiercely attacked him; they shot at him and pressed him hard. 24 Yet his bow remained taut, and his arms were made agile by the hands of the Mighty One of Jacob, by the name of the Shepherd, the Rock of Israel, 25 by the God of your father, who will help you, by the Almighty who will bless you with blessings of heaven above, blessings of the deep that lies beneath, blessings of the breasts and of the womb. 26 The blessings of your father are stronger than the blessings of the eternal mountains, the bounties of the everlasting hills; may they be on the head of Joseph, on the brow of him who was set apart from his brothers.

27 Benjamin is a ravenous wolf, in the morning devouring the prey, and at evening dividing the spoil.'

28 All these are the twelve tribes of Israel, and this is what their father said to them when he blessed them, blessing each one of them with a suitable blessing.

The second scene begins as Jacob gathers his sons around him. It does not sound either at the outset or as the text unfolds as if what Jacob is doing here is 'blessing' his sons. The opening words of Chapter 49 say that Jacob summoned his sons, to tell them what would happen to them in days to come. He then proceeds, in several cases, to predict trouble and woe. There is precious little 'blessing' apparently, in what he foresees for Reuben, who had 'defiled his father's bed' (compare Gen. 35:22): to him Jacob says 'you shall no longer excel' (verse 4). Similarly with Simeon and Levi, whose violent massacre of Shechem's city had made their father 'odious to the inhabitants of the land' (Gen. 34:30): to them Jacob says 'I will divide them' (verse 7). So far from blessing them, he actually curses their anger (verse 6). But the conclusion of the chapter could not be more emphatic: 'All these are the twelve tribes of Israel, and this is what their father said to them when he blessed them, blessing each one of them with a suitable blessing' (Gen. 49:28). The disparity between the way the text reads and the way the text is summarised is startling.

The other startling disparity is in the space afforded to each of the brothers. In death, as in life, Jacob does not treat his sons equally. The words addressed to Zebulun, Gad, Asher and

Naphtali (and, perhaps more surprisingly, Benjamin too) warrant barely a verse each. In keeping with his prominence in the story (and of course, the prominence of the tribe in the later history of Israel), Judah is afforded five verses (verses 8 to 12), all very positive: 'the sceptre shall not depart from Judah, nor the ruler's staff from between his feet' (verse 10).

But it is inevitably Joseph for whom Jacob reserves a special treatment. Two things stand out about the verses allocated to him (22–26). The first is that here alone in Jacob's speech, there is a reference to God (apart, that is, from the brief expression of praise in verse 18, not obviously connected to the words addressed to either Dan or Gad). When Jacob foresees the future of Reuben, Issachar and even Benjamin, for example, he does not foresee the presence of God. It is a shocking and unexpected absence. Whereas, in speaking of Joseph, he piles up the references to 'the Mighty One of Jacob', 'the Shepherd', 'the Rock of Israel', 'the God of your father', 'the Almighty'.

Secondly, and with some inevitability in terms of the narrative, it is only in connection with Joseph that Jacob actually blesses. The word 'blessing' doesn't occur except in verses 25 and 26. But there it occurs repeatedly: 'the Almighty will bless you, with the blessings of heaven above, blessings of the deep that lies beneath, blessings of the breasts and of the womb' (verse 25). These words are unparalleled in the Old Testament in the almost Celtic way in which they link blessing so specifically to particular aspects of God's creation. But Jacob isn't finished. He goes on, 'The blessings of your father are stronger than the blessings of the eternal mountains, the bounties of the everlasting hills: may they be on the head of Joseph, on the brow of him who was set apart from his brothers.'

Jacob's final act, then, is to 'bless' his sons. But he does it in the only way he knows. Just as he himself stole not only the birthright from his older brother Esau, but also their father's blessing (Gen. 27), so on his deathbed, he focuses his own blessing on his favourite, to the apparent exclusion of the others.

The others are provided for: they each have their allotment of the Promised Land; but Joseph is 'set apart'. There is an ambiguity about that phrase. Does Jacob mean that he himself set Joseph apart as his favourite (and broadcasted the fact in unsubtle ways, from the special coat at the start of Joseph's life to the special blessing at the end); or does he mean that Joseph was set apart by God, for the purpose of 'preserving life'? As elsewhere in this extended narrative, divine and human action are probably to be seen acting in concert here. It is characteristic of the grace of God that it acts even in concert with human folly and frailty – indeed, it has to; ultimately, no other kind of human action is available.

Chapter Fourteen

'Carry my Bones'

(Genesis 49:29 – 50:26)

Introduction

Seventeen years passed between the arrival of Jacob and his family in Egypt and his death at the age of one hundred and forty seven. In this final episode in the Joseph story, it transpires that that period was not necessarily a time of peace and harmony in the family, at least as Joseph's brothers experienced it. For when Jacob died, their fears about the true state of their relationship with their brother re-surfaced. It is really only in this last episode that a true reconciliation between them and Joseph is achieved.

There is often an assumption in the church that forgiveness is easily offered and reconciliation cheaply achieved. But perhaps this narrative holds out a more realistic model. Where a painful breach of trust has occurred, it can take a long time for a full and complete restoration to take place.

The Joseph story closes with two deaths, one elaborate burial and a final glimpse of the chronically complicated relationship between Joseph and his brothers. So the final episode in the narrative falls into four scenes. Scene One (Gen. 49:29–50.3) describes the death of Jacob; Scene Two describes his burial (Gen. 50:4–14); Scene Three describes the ultimate reconciliation between Joseph and his brothers (Gen. 50:15–21); and the final scene (Gen. 50:22–26) describes Joseph's own death.

Scene One: The Death of Jacob (Genesis 49:29 – 50:3)

> 49:29 Then he charged them, saying to them, 'I am about to be gathered to my people. Bury me with my ancestors – in the cave in the field of Ephron the Hittite, 30 in the cave in the field at Machpelah, near Mamre, in the land of Canaan, in the field that Abraham bought from Ephron the Hittite as a burial site. 31 There Abraham and his wife Sarah were buried; there Isaac and his wife Rebekah were buried; and there I buried Leah – 32 the field and the cave that is in it were purchased from the Hittites.' 33 When Jacob ended his charge to his sons, he drew up his feet into the bed, breathed his last, and was gathered to his people. 50:1 Then Joseph threw himself on his father's face and wept over him and kissed him. 2 Joseph commanded the physicians in his service to embalm his father. So the physicians embalmed Israel; 3 they spent forty days in doing this, for that is the time required for embalming. And the Egyptians wept for him seventy days.

The first scene in this, the last act in the drama of Joseph's life story, is the death of his father, Jacob. There is something deeply ironic about the first few verses of Chapter 50, and the end of Chapter 49 grows in significance in the light of them. What happens to Jacob immediately after his death could not be more Egyptian. He is embalmed. This is an Egyptian practice, not a Hebrew one. The text has emphasis: 'Joseph commanded the physicians in his service to embalm his father. So the physicians embalmed Israel' (Gen. 50:2). They mourn Jacob for seventy days. Again, this is an Egyptian mourning period, not a Hebrew one; and the 'they' who do the weeping is the Egyptians. It is a startling end for Israel, the father of the nation. He dies in Egypt and apparently as an Egyptian. His identity as recipient of the promises of God could hardly be more obscured. And the closing verses of Chapter 49 are to be read in that light. Jacob cares about what happens to his body. It's not a trivial thing for him, whether he is buried in Egypt or Canaan. It matters. And it matters because of God's promises to Jacob in relation to the people and the land. In death, Jacob is still holding on to those promises.

First, he binds his sons to the promise of God in relation to the people. The euphemism in Genesis 49:29 is telling: 'I am about to be gathered to my people.' Certainly there is nothing developed here in the way of a hope for life beyond death: but the phrase does imply that Jacob sees death as a restoration of relationships rather than as a severing of them – as a reunion. And he wants to be buried where his ancestors are buried as a symbol of that reunion. It's clear from Genesis 49:33 that the place of burial is only a symbolic and not a literal expression of that reunion. Long before his dying wish can be put into effect, the text says that 'When Jacob ended his charge to his sons, he drew up his feet into the bed, breathed his last, and was gathered to his people.' It's at the moment of his death, not at the moment of his burial, that Jacob is reunited with his forebears.

It's also worth noting that Jacob doesn't only want to be buried with his ancestors: he wants to be buried specifically where Abraham and Sarah (to whom the promise of land and nation was first given), Isaac and Rebecca (to whom the promise of land and nation was renewed) and Leah (though not Rachel) were buried. Jacob is not just looking back here: he is looking forward and reminding his sons of their inheritance as heirs of the promise of nationhood.

And similarly, he binds his sons to the promise of God in relation to the land. He doesn't just want to be buried with specifically named ancestors; he wants to be buried in a specific place – not just in the land of Canaan, but in the piece of Canaan which belongs to him and which amounts to a deposit on what is to come: the cave in the field of Ephron the Hittite (compare Gen. 23). Again there is emphasis in the text: the cave is mentioned three times in quick succession in verses 29 to 32 – and twice Jacob repeats the fact that the cave was purchased. It truly belongs to him. But again it matters as much for what it represents about the future as for what it represents about the past: the cave is Jacob's foothold in Canaan, a first instalment of what God has promised.

The hope in Jacob's last words is not evident at first – but here is one of the parts of the Joseph story which is tied closely to earlier chapters of Genesis, and especially Chapters 17 to 26, in which the promises of God are given to Jacob's father and grandfather.

Scene Two: The Burial of Jacob (Genesis 50:4–14)

> 4 When the days of weeping for him were past, Joseph addressed the household of Pharaoh, 'If now I have found favour with you, please speak to Pharaoh as follows: 5 My father made me swear an oath; he said, "I am about to die. In the tomb that I hewed out for myself in the land of Canaan, there you shall bury me." Now therefore let me go up, so that I may bury my father; then I will return.' 6 Pharaoh answered, 'Go up, and bury your father, as he made you swear to do.' 7 So Joseph went up to bury his father. With him went up all the servants of Pharaoh, the elders of his household, and all the elders of the land of Egypt, 8 as well as all the household of Joseph, his brothers, and his father's household. Only their children, their flocks, and their herds were left in the land of Goshen. 9 Both chariots and charioteers went up with him. It was a very great company. 10 When they came to the threshing floor of Atad, which is beyond the Jordan, they held there a very great and sorrowful lamentation; and he observed a time of mourning for his father seven days. 11 When the Canaanite inhabitants of the land saw the mourning on the threshing floor of Atad, they said, 'This is a grievous mourning on the part of the Egyptians.' Therefore the place was named Abel-mizraim; it is beyond the Jordan. 12 Thus his sons did for him as he had instructed them. 13 They carried him to the land of Canaan and buried him in the cave of the field at Machpelah, the field near Mamre, which Abraham bought as a burial site from Ephron the Hittite. 14 After he had buried his father, Joseph returned to Egypt with his brothers and all who had gone up with him to bury his father.

Scene Two describes the burial of Jacob in accordance with his wishes, 'in the cave of the field at Machpelah, the field near Mamre, which Abraham bought as a burial site from Ephron the Hittite.' Yet it does so without ever mentioning Jacob by name. He is, instead, Joseph's father. Eight times, these verses refer to him as 'my/your/his father', in a way that serves to link Joseph with the promises of God to his forebears.

As the Joseph story reaches its end and he is reunited with his brothers, his precedence in the family is assumed. It is Joseph, rather than Reuben, Simeon or Judah, who not only approaches

Pharaoh to make arrangements for the trip to Canaan, but who leads the company both out of Egypt (verse 7) and back again (verse 14) and who leads the time of mourning too (verse 10). (The indirect approach to Pharaoh is a little odd and unexpected here: Joseph's direct access to Pharaoh is taken for granted earlier in the story. Perhaps it reflects the fact that this is a personal and private matter, rather than a piece of official state business.) Whatever Joseph's brothers might have thought about his rightful place among them at the beginning of the story, they seem to accept his leadership at the end.

Again it is striking how 'Egyptian' the people of God have become: for all their independence in Goshen, they are evidently dependent on Pharaoh to make the trip into Canaan, and there is some emphasis placed on the need for Joseph and his brothers to return (verse 5). The dialogue between Joseph and Pharaoh has similarities with the later dialogue between Moses and Pharaoh in Exodus 5 – 10, leading up to the Exodus. When Moses seeks permission for the people of Israel to leave Egypt to observe a religious obligation (only in the wilderness, admittedly, but in the direction of Canaan) – permission is first refused, on the grounds that it is motivated only by Israelite laziness (Ex. 5:17). Later, Pharaoh suggests the Israelites might worship within Egypt (Ex. 8:25), or at least might not go very far (Ex. 8:28). Then, he concedes that the men may go, but not the women or children (Ex. 10:10); and finally that all the people can go, but not the flocks and herds (Ex. 10:24). The question is never raised in the Joseph story, whether the retinue leaving to mourn for Jacob might have included women, children and cattle – or how that prospect might have been viewed by Pharaoh. But perhaps the shadow of Israel's later enslavement has begun to fall over Jacob and his brothers: they can go, but only if they leave womenfolk and children, flocks and herds behind (verse 8), only under armed escort (verse 8; though of course at the time this will have been seen as being offered for the protection of the caravan) and only after the Egyptian fashion – to the extent that the mourning is regarded by the Canaanite observers as 'a mourning of the Egyptians'. Perhaps most ironically of all, Jacob's only foothold in Canaan (or at least, a neighbouring site east of the Jordan), acquires a new name: *Abel-Mizraim*. From that time onwards it would be identified with reference to Egypt ('Mizraim' being its Hebrew name).

Despite their exemption from the enslavement in Chapter 47, it is hard to escape the impression that the family of Israel are no longer quite free: they are increasingly beholden to Pharaoh and their Egyptian hosts, so that when Joseph 'returned to Egypt with his brothers and all who had gone up with him to bury his father', it's clear they would not be leaving again any time soon.

Scene Three: The Fear of Joseph's Brothers (Gen. 50:15–21)

> 15 Realising that their father was dead, Joseph's brothers said, 'What if Joseph still bears a grudge against us and pays us back in full for all the wrong that we did to him?' 16 So they approached Joseph, saying, 'Your father gave this instruction before he died, 17 "Say to Joseph: I beg you, forgive the crime of your brothers and the wrong they did in harming you." Now therefore please forgive the crime of the servants of the God of your father.' Joseph wept when they spoke to him. 18 Then his brothers also wept, fell down before him, and said, 'We are here as your slaves.' 19 But Joseph said to them, 'Do not be afraid! Am I in the place of God? 20 Even though you intended to do harm to me, God intended it for good, in order to preserve a numerous people, as he is doing today. 21 So have no fear; I myself will provide for you and your little ones.' In this way he reassured them, speaking kindly to them.

Despite the seventeen years of their sojourn in Egypt, the relationship between Joseph and his brothers remains precarious, to say the least. With Jacob dead, the brothers are afraid that Joseph will now show his true colours and exact from them some terrible retribution for their act – now almost forty years previously – in selling him into slavery. They fear that it has only been out of reverence for Jacob that Joseph has treated them so reasonably for so long. 'What if Joseph still bears a grudge against us', they ask each other, 'and pays us back in full for all the wrong we did to him?' So they decide to approach Joseph, to seek his full and final forgiveness.

It is a sad moment in the story. It is sad firstly, because the brothers had evidently been living in Joseph's presence for seventeen years, without any assurance that he had forgiven them. It is sad, secondly, because they are not able to approach him directly and in their own voice, as it were. They not only send him a message (which in itself implies a certain continued distance between them and him), but they feel the need to put their plea in Jacob's mouth. And it's sad thirdly, because (whether or not Jacob said anything of the kind – given his special propensity for manoeuvring, it's quite possible he did suggest such a step), when they relate their father's wish to their brother, they call Jacob, 'Your father'. Not 'our father' – 'yours'. The word seems loaded with all the baggage of Jacob's favouritism towards Joseph. Those wounds went deep.

But their plea brings the best – absolutely the best – out of Joseph. His reaction is worth noting in detail. First, when he receives their message, he cries (verse 17). Actually, the adult Joseph was prone to tears. It's hard to imagine that was also the mark of the youth. He has learned tears through his sufferings (the Christian reader is reminded of the experience of Jesus: Heb. 5:7–8). Seven times in Chapters 42 to 50, Joseph weeps: first, when his brothers acknowledge their fault in relation to his sale into slavery (42:24); again when he sees Benjamin for the first time (43:30); again (twice) when he reveals himself to his brothers (45:2,14–15); again, when he is reunited with his father (46:29); again, at the start of this final act of the drama, when his father dies (50:1); and then again, for the last time in the story, at this point. Tears in Joseph's life, as so often in ours, and especially in church life, are a good sign.

His brothers then come into his presence: they bow (a final fulfilment of Joseph's youthful dream) and offer themselves as his slaves. Both this offer and Joseph's tears echo the day that Joseph first revealed himself to his brothers. But their offer prompts Joseph to make one of the most mature, moving, and godly speeches in the whole drama. First, he refuses either to judge his brothers or to exact vengeance: 'Don't be afraid', he says to them, 'Am I in the place of God?' It is always a mark of holiness, when a person feels wronged and yet is able to leave judgment and vengeance to God. Then, he affirms the providence of God with regard to the past and the present: he confronts explicitly the fact that they may have done what they did in order to harm him, but underlines that beyond their malicious purpose was the benevolent purpose of God: 'God intended it for good, in order to preserve a numerous people, as he is doing today.' And then, in verse 21, he pledges his support for them in the future. Of all the glimpses we are given into the character of Joseph, this is perhaps the most positive. At the very moment of the fulfilment of his youthful dream, he is most changed from his youthful self. Here Joseph comes across as magnanimous, compassionate and tender. However gifted the teenage version may have been, there wasn't much that was 'kind' about him.

Scripture repeatedly affirms that God has a good plan and purpose not only for creation (Rom. 8:28), and for 'his people' (Jer. 29:11), but for individuals too (Ps. 57:2; 138:8; Prov. 16:9; 19:21). But it is important to note that Joseph's trust in God's good purpose for his life is not a naïve, unrealistic, romantic assumption of ease and prosperity. His confession of faith is not an expectation, lately so popular in some evangelical circles, that God will bless with worldly success those who hope in him. It is true that Joseph is, at this point in his story, rich and powerful – but his statement that God intended the harm that others did to him 'for good' is not a claim that God blesses with good those who are wrongly harmed by others. It is a claim that the malice of others was turned by God not just into blessing for Joseph, but so that Joseph might be a blessing to others. God worked blessing not just through the evil that was done to Joseph, but also through Joseph's own weaknesses and failings. It is a great reassurance to know that God is able to turn to blessing even the least worthy thoughts and deeds of his servants – and of the church.

Preachers are prone to see Joseph as a type of Christ at many points. Perhaps here the prefiguring is at its most poignant: Joseph suffers; and in his vindication, he rejoices not so much in his own circumstances, as in the 'salvation' his experience has brought to others.

Scene Four: The Death of Joseph (Genesis 50:22–26)

22 So Joseph remained in Egypt, he and his father's household; and Joseph lived one hundred and ten years. 23 Joseph saw Ephraim's

children of the third generation; the children of Machir son of Manasseh were also born on Joseph's knees. 24 Then Joseph said to his brothers, 'I am about to die; but God will surely come to you, and bring you up out of this land to the land that he swore to Abraham, to Isaac, and to Jacob.' 25 So Joseph made the Israelites swear, saying, 'When God comes to you, you shall carry up my bones from here.' 26 And Joseph died, being one hundred and ten years old; he was embalmed and placed in a coffin in Egypt.

There is something profound, also, about the fact that the story of Joseph moves so swiftly to its conclusion after the climax of the previous scene. Scholars have noted that the account of his death has a formal pattern to it: a 'chiasmus'. There is a movement from 'Egypt' to 'one hundred and ten years' to 'God will come to you' in verses 22–24; and from 'When God comes to you' to 'one hundred and ten years' to 'Egypt' in verses 25–26 (On 'chiasmus', compare chapter 6, page 52, Gen. 41:54–57).

These few verses apparently summarise (almost) half Joseph's life: we are invited to suppose that in the previous scene, at the time of his encounter with his brothers in 50:15–12, Joseph was fifty-six years old (17 + 22 + 17); here he dies at one hundred and ten. Perhaps his relationship with his brothers prospered in those years. Certainly the size of his family did: he lived to see not only his grandchildren, but his great-grandchildren (through Manasseh) and his great-great-grandchildren (through Ephraim).

The final words of the Joseph story are poignant. The drama closes with the protagonist not just dead, but 'embalmed and placed in a coffin in Egypt'. Already in the Joseph story, the question arises, how God's promise of 'a land' to Abraham, Isaac and Jacob can be fulfilled. Abraham and Isaac at least lived as aliens in Canaan, even if they never possessed it. Jacob also lived in Canaan, but had to leave it, driven by famine to join Joseph in Egypt. But he lived most of his days in the land promised by God to his family; and at least his bones were duly returned to his family burial place. Joseph's were not. Unlike his father, he lived most of his days in Egypt not Canaan; and unlike his father, he was buried 'in a coffin in Egypt'. At the end of the story of Joseph, the promises of God are about as far from being fulfilled as it is possible for them to be.

But Joseph dies in hope. His hope is in God – the God who 'will surely come' to his people but, not necessarily in a God who will do so within his own lifetime. Quite the opposite in fact: his hope that 'God will come to you ['my descendants', presumably, rather than 'my brothers'] and bring you up out of this land.' As with his father Jacob in Scene One (i.e., Gen. 49:29), what happens to his body matters because of his hope. It is for this reason that he pleads with his brothers and the Israelites for his bones to be taken up out of Egypt at the time of God's coming. And it is because this request is invested with theological significance, that the Scriptures are careful to note, in the sequel to this story, that his descendants honoured his dying plea. Moses ensured the bones of his ancestor were not left in Egypt (Ex. 13:19); and Joshua ensured their safe passage into Canaan, where they were buried 'at Shechem, in the portion of ground that Jacob had bought from the children of Hamor, the father of Shechem, for one hundred pieces of money' (Josh. 24:32; compare Gen. 33:19). In other words, as the book of Hebrews has it, it was 'by faith' that 'Joseph, at the end of his life, made mention of the exodus of the Israelites and gave instructions about his burial' (Heb. 11:22).

Concluding Reflections

When the present is grim, the question of the future becomes pressing. It is natural to seek assurance that all will be well. Joseph himself, his father and brothers (at various points), the cupbearer and the baker, and Pharaoh himself all lay hold of the future, seeking some indication that relief is at hand. It should come as no surprise to us if the church, in today's climate, is driven to do the same. To the extent that the church today operates in a demanding and sometimes a hostile context, it is understandable if it responds by looking for signs that tomorrow will bring prosperity and ease. If that is the case, it may be as well to return to the Joseph narrative as a whole, to consider what guidance it has to offer in this respect.

The Joseph Story: A Text for Tomorrow

The revelation of the future in the Joseph story is worth pondering. It is easy to suppose that today would be more bearable if we only knew what tomorrow held. If we only knew whether this illness would pass or that job be worth applying for, whether this mortgage would be affordable or that school be right for our children, how much more fully we could live today and how much more effectively we could seize the present moment. If we only knew what the outcome will be of this financial crisis or that controversy – how much easier it would be for the church to make good decisions today and to act rightly.

But a moment's thought tells us it isn't so. The misconception is neatly illustrated by the Joseph cycle. Uncertainty about tomorrow can distract us from our calling to make the most of today – but so can too specific a certainty. It is enough to know that tomorrow is in God's hands.

In the first half of the drama, the revelation of the future relates basically to the three pairs of dreams: those dreamt by Joseph in Chapter 37 (in which he learns early that one day his family will bow down to him); by the cupbearer and baker in Chapter 40 (in which they learn what will happen to them imminently); and by Pharaoh in Chapter 41 (in which he learns that seven years of fat and seven of famine are coming). But these revelations tend (at least in the cases of Joseph and Pharaoh) to increase, rather than decrease, the challenges which the characters in the drama face. In Joseph's case, the dreams tell him that one day (he is given no detail about when) he will rule over his family (he is given no detail about how). The dreams give no hint of the tortuous path he will have to take before his destiny is fulfilled. The dreams surely do not make his sufferings easier to bear; quite possibly, they make them harder. In prison his dreams must have seemed to mock, rather than sustain him. In Pharaoh's case, the dreams only reveal 'what is about to take place' in the sense that they spell out the nature of the impending crisis. They don't tell him what the outcome of the crisis will be or how he is to manage it. The dreams don't relieve him of the need to take action; on the contrary, they heighten his responsibility. (It may be that the cupbearer is an exception here: perhaps Joseph's interpretation of his dream made his last three days in prison more bearable; presumably the same cannot be said for the baker . . .)

Joseph in particular has been an inspiration to later generations of God's people. It is worth pausing to consider why this is. It is perhaps not because he was given, through his dreams, a privileged insight into the future. In some circles, this may have made him a spiritual giant to venerate, emulate or envy; it probably hasn't made him an encouragement and inspiration. Where Joseph has been an inspiration, it is partly because he trusted that the future belongs to God, even when his present circumstances belied it; and partly because he acted decisively in the present in such a way as to shape the future. Both his trust in God and his boldness in action are all the more inspiring, in view of his dreams – which might easily have led him either to despair of

God in anger and bitterness, or to forsake his obligations in indo-
lence and complacency. By the same token, Joseph is a challenge
to the church today in the face of a potentially difficult future, to
combine trust in God on the one hand with courageous action on
the other.

In the second half of the drama, the revelation of the future
relates to what is promised to Jacob. In his youth (Gen.
28:13–14), Jacob/Israel had been promised by God firstly, that
the land on which he was lying (Canaan) would be given to him
and to his descendants, secondly, that his descendants would be
as numerous as 'the dust of the earth' and thirdly that 'all the
families of the earth' would be blessed in him and his offspring.
In Genesis 46, in 'visions of the night' (the nearest thing that the
second half of the Joseph cycle has to a dream), God gives Jacob
a glimpse of the future – enough to reassure him that those earlier promises will be fulfilled. 'I will make of you a great nation
[in Egypt]. I myself will go down with you and I will bring you
up again. And Joseph's own hand shall close your eyes.' This
seems more specific. Certainly, it is easy to imagine that the
promise that he would not die before being reunited with his
long lost son would have made the journey to Egypt more man-
ageable. Indeed, as we saw in the commentary, it is from this
point in the narrative onwards that Jacob's spirit revives and his
hope returns.

But parts of this specific promise are not fulfilled – at least in
their most obvious sense. If within his own latter years Jacob's
family grew significantly into the great nation it would eventually become, the text does not say so. And God did not 'bring him
up again'. That is to say: if Jacob formed the impression from his
vision, that he and the great nation of his offspring would return
to Canaan to take possession of it in his lifetime, he was mistaken. On the other hand, it's not clear that Jacob did form that
impression. Such is the sense of solidarity from one generation to
the next in biblical thought, that Jacob seems content that the
promise applies equally to his offspring as to himself. On his
death bed, certainly, there is no hint of any disappointment in
Jacob, no hint of complaint that God has let him down or reneged
on his promises. Jacob and Joseph after him both die in hope, still
trusting in the promises of God.

This capacity to hope for what we may not see in our own generation is something the church needs desperately to recover. Contemporary western culture is acutely individualistic and impatient. Solidarities of all sorts have been eroded, not least those of family. And a capitalist economy cultivates an expectation that all things are possible now, from instant coffee to instant credit. The church colludes in this individualism and impatience. In particular, much of the response to the crises of decline and disunity in the church today may be unduly anxious for an immediate remedy. The clamour for both swift growth and a speedy resolution of controversy perhaps owes more to the culture of contemporary business life than to that of the Scriptures.

The story of Joseph offers the church of today great hope for tomorrow. Of course it does. But it does so simply by offering a robust affirmation that the future belongs to God. It is 'fixed by God'. This is enough to free God's people from agitation and fretfulness about what the future will bring. But the story of Joseph offers precious little detail in advance to its characters about either what this good future will look like, or when it will come to pass. The result is, that the hope generated for tomorrow fuels action today in bringing that future to pass.

The Joseph Story: A Text for Today

If the Joseph story offers the church only a very general hope as 'a text for tomorrow', it is much more specific as 'a text for today'. What sort of action do the characters in this narrative take, as they seek to shape their future? How do Joseph and his family behave and what can the church today learn from their examples? One set of actions relates to the adversities that the characters face; the other relates to the disharmony between them.

In relation to adversity, part of the point of the story is the maturing of Joseph, which takes place between Chapters 37 and 50, as he comes to terms with his trials. His growth as a person in the likeness of God is not swift or straightforward. Some very attractive characteristics emerge quite early in the story (a certain integrity in his dealings with Potiphar's wife in Chapter 39; a flair for responsibility in Chapters 39 and 40; a concern for the welfare

of others in Chapter 40); but some pretty unattractive characteristics remain quite late (his cat and mouse manipulation of his
brothers in Chapters 42 – 44; his ruthless oppression of the
Egyptian populace in Chapter 47). On the other hand, there is no
denying the development. The kindness and generosity he
demonstrates in the final chapter plainly represent a considerable
sanctification, relative to his brash self-righteousness at the outset of the narrative. Moreover, when Joseph acts well, especially
in Potiphar's house and in jail, it is not because there is an obvious advantage to him in doing so. This is how godliness is
formed in us. When we do the right thing, just because it is the
right thing to do, we co-operate with God's grace and are
changed into his likeness.

Similarly with the brothers, and especially Judah. They are still
blundering about in fearfulness by the end of the story, it is true.
But it is a genuinely penitent fearfulness. Led by Judah, who
learnt a harsh lesson in penitence in Chapter 38, the brothers
grow to acknowledge their faults and crimes. One of the refresh-
ing aspects of the narrative is just how little blaming there is in it.
Joseph doesn't blame his brothers for what they did to him; the
brothers barely blame one another; even Jacob grows out of that
tendency by the end of his life. A church (or a party in the church)
which is prone to blaming others is not a penitent church.

Jacob and his sons (the whole family of God's people) feel their
way forwards as the story unfolds, in compassion, mercy and
grace. They don't by any means always succeed. The narrative
makes no attempt to cover over their lapses: rather, it invites us
to reflect on the damage done by Jacob's favouritism, for example, or Joseph's manoeuvrings and machinations. The points at
which they fail to trust in God are laid before the reader as well
as the points at which they are faithful.

In all these ways, the reader sees that the adversities the characters face are not merely negative experiences. By the grace of
God they become the means, by which 'life is preserved' and
godliness nurtured. Holiness comes less through dramatic experiences of God's Spirit, than through the faithful endurance of trials. We grow in likeness to God just by pressing on, day after day,
in the ordinary and unglamorous demands of life, in obedience
and love.

In relation to the disharmony between the brothers and between Jacob and his sons, the lessons have already been drawn in the course of the commentary. The road to reconciliation is a long and winding one. None of the parties is perfect: now the brothers shame Joseph by their contrition and capacity for sacrifice; now he shows them the way forward in kindness and generosity; now they show themselves fearful and despairing, now he proves controlling and manipulative. But the parties do not give up on one another either, and in the end a hard won reconciliation is achieved. The western church today may perceive itself here as in a mirror.

Meanwhile, in their journey towards reconciliation, Joseph and the members of his family become a blessing to others: to Potiphar, the jailer, the cupbearer, Pharaoh and to Egypt. It is as though, as they gradually address their differences, Jacob, Joseph and his brothers become mediators of God's goodness to those who are still more different from themselves. The hope must be, where the church in the West today is concerned, that it will not lose sight of its calling to bless those outside itself; and indeed that in the way it handles its internal divisions it will become more sensitive, and not less, to the concerns and needs of the outsider.

In the face of decline, then, it is obvious that the church will long and pray and plan for growth in numbers. In our longing, praying and planning for growth however, we should not underestimate the benefits that are to be gained from adversity on the one hand, and from walking the long and winding road towards reconciliation on the other.

> *Then grant us grace, Companion-God*
> *To choose again the pilgrim's way*
> *And help us to accept with joy*
> *The challenge of tomorrow's day.*

'Now let us from this table rise,' Common Praise, 315. Fred Kaan © 1968, reproduced with permission, Stainer and Bell Ltd.

Joseph Wise and Otherwise

The intersection of Wisdom and Covenant in Genesis 37 – 50

Lindsay Wilson

This book studies how wisdom ideas in Genesis 37 – 50 relate to the themes and motifs that emerge from the Abrahamic promises. While the Joseph narrative is not simply a wisdom tale, there appear to be many features that are suggestive of wisdom. A literary reading of the chapters examines how these 'wisdom-like elements' relate to the story as a whole. Chapter 37 establishes that God will cause Joseph to rise to prominence. The intriguing story of Tamar in chapter 38 is seen as a kind of microcosm of the entire Joseph story, with Tamar securing life, justice and reconciliation through her wise initiatives, leading ultimately to the preservation of the line of promise. Joseph's public use of wisdom is considered in chapters 39 – 41, where he uses power successfully and with discernment. Joseph's private use of wisdom occupies chapters 42 – 45, as Joseph brings about change in his brothers and extends forgiveness to them. Chapters 46 – 50 complete the story by weaving the concerns of the previous chapters into the fabric of God's purposes for his covenant people. In the final form of the narrative, both the wisdom and the covenant strands are seen to be prominent. The covenant strand is reflected in the connections forged with the rest of Genesis, and the wider Pentateuch. The wisdom strand is evident in the public and private arenas, as well as in Joseph's tested character. God's behind-the-scenes activity, coupled with human initiatives, emerges as another 'wisdom-like element'. Both covenant and wisdom retain their distinctive contributions, and are complementary ways of God establishing his active rule. God uses wise human initiatives to accomplish his overarching purposes

978-1-84227-140-7